FL.   .~r~ NO.4

The Flashback series is sponsored by the
European Ethnological Research Centre,
c/o the National Museums of Scotland,
Queen Street, Edinburgh EH2 1JD.

General Editor: Alexander Fenton

Other books by Ian MacDougall:

Minutes of Edinburgh Trades Council, 1859–1873
  (ed.) (1969)
A Catalogue of some Labour Records in Scotland and
  some Scots Records outside Scotland (1978)
Essays in Scottish Labour History (ed.) (1978)
Militant Miners (1981)
Labour in Scotland: A Pictorial History from the
  Eighteenth Century to the Present Day (1985)
Voices from the Spanish Civil War (1986)
The Prisoners at Penicuik, 1803–1814 (1989)
Voices from the Hunger Marches (2 vols) (1990–1991)
Hard Work, Ye Ken (1993)
Hoggie's Angels (1995)

Forthcoming:
Voices from War

MUNGO MACKAY
and the
GREEN TABLE

Newtongrange Miners Remember

Ian MacDougall

Tuckwell Press
in association with
Midlothian District Council

First published in 1995 by
Tuckwell Press Ltd
The Mill House
Phantassie
East Linton
East Lothian EH40 3DG
Scotland

ISBN 1 898410 66 6

British Library Cataloguing-in-Publication Data
A Catalogue record for this book
is available on request from the
British Library

The publisher gratefully acknowledges subsidy of the Scottish
Arts Council for the publication of this book

Typeset by Hewer Text Composition Services, Edinburgh
Printed and bound by Cromwell Press, Melksham, Wiltshire

CONTENTS

FOREWORD

There was a certain style of management which in the late twentieth century has nearly disappeared from British industry. Power, almost dictatorial power, was identified with one individual. The personality, the decisions of that individual dominated lives and communities in a total way. In many cases the individual concerned was the owner as well as manager of a forge or factory. In the coal industry it was often the agent whose personality loomed over a community and workforce. Mungo Mackay, agent and general manager to the Lothian Coal Company, was just such an individual.

These voices which have been gathered by Ian MacDougall are a record of what it was like to be on the receiving end of such a management. It is a male world centred upon work with the pride and humiliations of the wage relationship. Mackay was both feared and admired. He was clearly a very good mining engineer and the men knew this. He was at the cutting edge of capitalism, negotiating the prices and conditions that determined profits. He was also a tough manager who shared his authority with no-one. Behind the green table in the company office he was judge, jury and legislator.

His power was constructed in a total and careful manner. It required the men's respect for his own skill, but this was only part of the story. The power of the green table with its decisions and discipline that affected the lives and well being of individuals and families was part of a social arrangement which historians have called 'paternalism'. The power of the employer over the labour force was not limited to the cash element of the wage but extended to other aspects of life. In Newtongrange, Mackay controlled all the housing. This sort of control has a long history in Scotland going back to Robert Owen's factory settlement in New Lanark. It was widespread in the rural areas of Scotland where until very recently most housing was controlled by the farmers and landlords. Linen mills like that at Prinlaws in Fife, villages linked to stone and slate quarries as well as the iron and steel producing settlements around Motherwell were all places in which the employer controlled the housing. This control could extend in many ways. Thus Mackay controlled the cooperative store, the parish council and even the Dean Tavern. Remember that before the Local Government Act of 1929, the parish council had a central place in welfare provision, thus it was vital that Mackay could control its operations. This system gave employers great power because an argument over work involved not just the loss of wages or work but the potential loss of house and social life. The system worked for several reasons. Those who lived and worked in Newtongrange often found it difficult to imagine any alternative, at least any alternative that was better than that offered by Mackay. The system depended on an unspoken bargain. In return for wages and total subservience the people of Newtongrange got housing and regular work. The housing was well maintained and probably better than that occupied by most miners in Scotland. Those who stayed in favour with Mackay could expect work for as long as the pit lasted. Older men were often given lighter jobs around the pit shaft.

The power of the green table died for two reasons. The strengthening of tenants' rights and rent legislation plus the availability of local authority housing from the late 1940s onwards meant that the coal companies no longer had a monopoly of local housing. After 1947, when coal was nationalised, power was removed not just from private owners but also from their local agents. Power went with a position in the National Coal Board hierarchy, not with the individual personality. The same thing happened in many industries in the 1950s as closures and takeovers removed power from a locality and an individual to corporate head-quarters in both public and private sector. Increasingly fear no longer came from the green table but from the remote, impersonal agency of the corporate plan with its restructuring and redundancy notices.

The world of work in the coal industry was a very male world. The power of Mackay created many difficulties. Male industrial traditions built up over the nineteenth century had insisted on the separation of home life and work. The miner's subordination at work was matched by his authority at home. Mackay compromised this by his power over the houses and even the domestic behaviour of families. Mackay's power also limited the possibility of politics. With the exception of the great national strikes of 1921 and 1926 there were few stoppages at the pit. Union activity was low-key and at times seemed to have been incorporated into the management authority structure of the pit. Anyone interested in party politics and socialism had to go quietly into Dalkeith. This was very different from the so-called 'little Moscows' in the Fife mining area. One of the few mentions of politics comes from a man who had work experience outside the village and from another man who began work after 1945 and hence had his views formed by the experience of nationalisation in 1947. This dictatorial, personal industrial authority is often identi-fied with the nineteenth century and it will surprise many that it lasted so long. Whatever judgement the reader passes on this system, it should not be identified with a free market. A free market depends upon choice and information. New-tongrange may have been a 'model village' for many but there was little choice. Mackay had the monopoly of jobs and houses. He also ensured that men rarely knew what each other was earning, especially in the white collar and technical grades.

If you go into Newtongrange today you will find that the green table has returned as part of a museum display. Mackay's ghostly voice (spoken by an actor) presides over the tableau. It is a well designed piece of theatre. The complexity of managing and working in Newtongrange has become an accessible melodrama surrounded by the restored hulks of surviving machinery. No doubt Mackay would be astonished to find that his life's work had become part of a good day out. Presentations like this are now very common. They make the confrontations of Mackay and his miners in some ways more accessible. I guess there were no school trips in the 1930s to witness and pass judgement upon his disciplining of the miners. At the same time it makes the confrontations more remote. They are in the 'past' where they can be viewed with safety. The voices of the men recorded in this book are an essential part of a world which is at once very familiar and very different from the world of work and home in the 1990s.

Bob Morris
Economic and Social History
Edinburgh University

INTRODUCTION

Mungo Mackay and the Green Table flourished not in medieval times but in the first half of the twentieth century. Mackay, as agent and general manager of the Lothian Coal Company based at Newtongrange in Midlothian, dominated the lives of the miners employed by the Company there and in several nearby pits from the 1890s until his retirement and death on the eve of the Second World War.

Mackay's domination was not confined to the miners at their work. Most of the Lothian Coal Company's miners and their families lived in the Company's tied houses at Newtongrange and Rosewell. So, as the recollections below make clear, that domination extended to the miners and their families at home. So extensive and enduring indeed was that domination that even yet, more than half a century after his death in 1939, the belief (or, at least, the saying) survives among some older residents at Newtongrange that 'Mungo's no' deid yet.'

What it meant to live and work under the regime of Mungo Mackay and the Lothian Coal Company is told in these recollections by miners and others. The recollections are, with two partial exceptions (those of Pat Flynn and Tommy Kerr), first-hand accounts by employees of the Company in Mackay's day. They form an oral history of the subject that is not least valuable since few written records of the Lothian Coal Company, and no papers of Mungo Mackay himself, seem to survive.

Mungo Mackay, a brilliant mining engineer from Ayrshire, where he was born in 1867 and had worked first at Auchinleck colliery before moving to Polton pit, Midlothian, about 1894, was a tyrannical manager. His tyranny was not unique in the Scottish coal industry in the half-century before nationalisation in 1947, but his ruthless exercise of it over such a lengthy period made him notorious among miners even in coalfields beyond the Lothians. His tyrannical domination of the miners and their families rested upon a systematic and comprehensive system of industrial and social control of which the witnesses below provide many examples. 'He says to me one day,' "Ye'll do what ye're told or ah'll put ye out your house"', recalls the late James 'Treacle' Moffat. 'So ah says, "Well, ye'll just have to put ez out the house." Ah says, "Ah've a good home tae go tae." "Aye," he says, "if ye gane back to yer faither and mither we'll pit them out the house too."' And the late James Reid, for many years a wages clerk in the office of the Lothian Coal Company at Newtongrange, recalls: 'I remember one miner who had been called up in front o' the Green Table. He had been off his work. It was the old tale: they'd taken that much off in off-takes that they had left the chap wi' about five shillins—25 pence. Mungo Mackay came down the stairs and this miner followed him and he was sobbin'. He was askin' Mackay, "How can ah keep my wife and my children off five shillins a week?" And Mackay told him: "Get out! Out!"'

Some of the witnesses below recall a very different experience with Mackay. 'He wis good tae me,' says Lewis Morrison, a mining surveyor with the Lothian Coal Company. 'Mrs Mackay always asked hoo ah wis gettin' on. And I think he just sort o' kept a wee bit eye on me. He took quite a fatherly interest in me, oh, he definitely did.'

These recollections cover a wide range of aspects of life and work in the coal pits and mining villages concerned. Conditions of labour, wages and working hours, safety, housing, health and sickness, poverty, diet, Lithuanian immigrant workers, mining trade unionism, religion and the church, freemasonry, industrial accidents and deaths, miners' strikes and lock-outs, local sporting rivalries, and the isolation but strong sense of community of the mining villages, are among those aspects recalled.

Although he began work a few years after the death of Mungo Mackay, Pat Flynn grew up in Rosewell—known as 'Little Ireland'—three miles south-west of Newtongrange as the crow flies, and recalls vividly how extensive and tight a grip the Lothian Coal Company exercised upon his village and its miners. 'In Rosewell,' he tells us, 'the pit wis owned by the Lothian Coal Company. The Tavern, where you had your pint o' beer, wis owned by the Lothian Coal Company. The Co-operative Store . . . it belonged to the Lothian Coal Company. The chemist's belonged to the Company store . . . And . . . the biggest thing o' the bloody lot the Lothian Coal Company owned, wis the houses . . . The Lothian Coal Company they owned ye really, body and soul.'

An effective intelligence system that made use of informers in pit and village, a virtual reign of terror practised by Mungo Mackay at his Green Table, fear of eviction from Company housing, and fear of unemployment in an era when, as one veteran below recalls, 'There were always another man at the gate ready to take over your job': these were among the factors that made Mungo Mackay and his Green Table a byword among miners not only in the Lothians but in other coalfields, too.

It was in a chance remark by that veteran Fife militant miner the late John McArthur of Buckhaven during an extended interview I had with him quarter of a century ago that I first learned of Mungo Mackay and the Green Table. I resolved then to try to explore the subject once time permitted. The opportunity came in the early 1980s with an invitation from Billy Kay to contribute programmes to his BBC Radio Scotland oral history series *Odyssey*. Based on several interviews with veteran miners and other villagers of Newtongrange, *Mungo Mackay and the Green Table* was first broadcast in 1982. Since then I have interviewed from time to time others with first-hand recollections of Mungo Mackay and his regime, and also conducted more extensive interviews with some of my original interviewees, such as the late James Reid. The recollections below are therefore more comprehensive than those on which the radio programme was based, and very much more so than the brief selected extracts from the earlier interviews I had undertaken in 1981–82 that were published in the latter year in the second volume of *Odyssey*, edited by Billy Kay.

In presenting these recollections an attempt has been made throughout to preserve the actual words of all those interviewed, subject of course to necessary transpositions to ensure coherence and to deletions of irrelevant or repetitious matter.

For practical help or encouragement I am indebted to many people. The debt is especially great to all those who allowed me to interview them and record their recollections. It is sad that Adam Haldane, James 'Treacle' Moffat, John Telfer, William Taylor, James Reid, Alexander Trench, Peter Herriot, Bill Steele, George Weston and Tommy Thomson have died before seeing their recollections in print. I am grateful also to District Councillor James Green, and to Elaine Donald, Marilyn Rorison, Janice Dagg, Colin McLean, Mike Ashworth, George Archibald, Marion Richardson, Alan Reid, and John Tuckwell. My greatest debt is, as always, to my wife Sandra.

Ian MacDougall
March 1995

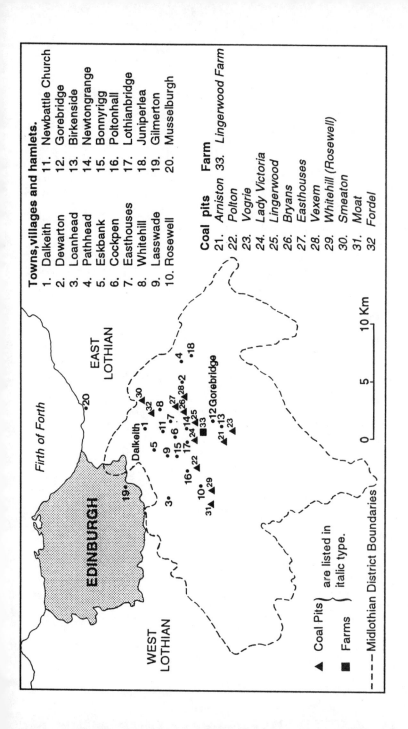

Towns, villages and hamlets.

1. Dalkeith
2. Dewarton
3. Loanhead
4. Pathhead
5. Eskbank
6. Cockpen
7. Easthouses
8. Whitehill
9. Lasswade
10. Rosewell
11. Newbattle Church
12. Gorebridge
13. Birkenside
14. Newtongrange
15. Bonnyrigg
16. Poltonhall
17. Lothianbridge
18. Juniperlea
19. Gilmerton
20. Musselburgh

Coal pits   Farm

21. Arniston   33. *Lingerwood Farm*
22. Polton
23. Vogrie
24. Lady Victoria
25. Lingerwood
26. Bryans
27. Easthouses
28. Vexem
29. Whitehill (Rosewell)
30. Smeaton
31. Moat
32 Fordel

Firth of Forth

EAST LOTHIAN

EDINBURGH

WEST LOTHIAN

Dalkeith

Gorebridge

10 Km

▲ Coal Pits ⎫ are listed in
■ Farms ⎬ italic type.
⎭

– – – Midlothian District Boundaries

ARCHIE WILSON

I am a retired miner and I come from Newtongrange. I spent practically all my life working in the Lady Victoria colliery there.

My first acquaintance with Mr Mungo Mackay was in 1912 when I was a boy. The pit was on strike at that time[1] My father, being a bricklayer with the Lothian Coal Company, had no work underground and Mr Mackay got my father, along with a Mr Hughes, to build a wall seven feet high round his big house just opposite the Lady Victoria pit.

On the day that I met Mr Mackay I was taking up my father's dinner. Mr Mackay appeared on the scene and conversed wi' ma dad and then he asked me: 'Oh, you are Ralph Wilson's son?' I said, 'Yes, I am, sir.' In these days we were learned to call our elders in a better position 'sir', which we thought nothing about then. He asked me the reason I was there. Telling him what I was there for, he asked me if I had been at school. I said I hadn't been at school and he gave me a quarrelin'. He asked me what I wanted to do when I left school. And of course I told him. 'Well,' I says, 'I'd like to be a bricklayer like my father.' He says, 'Well, if you do so and study you'll perhaps be a good bricklayer some day.' That was my first experience with Mr Mackay.

From that date I did not see Mr Mackay for quite a long time—in fact, until the 1914–18 War started. My father died in 1915 and Mr Mackay sent his condolences to my mother. Six weeks later my elder brother, who had been the engineman at the Vexem pit at Newtongrange, was killed in the Dardanelles.[2] On that occasion Mr Mackay came to our house to see my mother and asked my mother what she was going to do with me, as I was then thirteen years of age. My bereaved mother said I would have to work as I was the only breadwinner left in the family. So my mother got an exemption for me from the school to start work in 1915.

Now at that time, during these War years, the dependants in Newtongrange of the miners who served in the Forces paid no rent to the Lothian Coal Company, which owned the houses. Mr Mackay had arranged this through Mr James A. Hood, the owner of the Company, that people who were willing to sacrifice their lives for their country were entitled to free rent for the time that they were in the Forces. They paid no rent, no gas, no taxes whatever during their service in the Forces.[3]

Mr Mackay made arrangements for me to see him and in 1915 I went up to his office. I wanted an apprenticeship but Mr Mackay told me it was not possible at that time. So I started on the pithead as a boy of thirteen years of age at the Lady Victoria colliery. My wage at that time was 1/10d. per day. I was then known as a coupler. I was coupling hutches together before they went to the cage.

I did not see Mr Mackay very much at that time but knew that he was on the pithead every day of his life, looking round the workings and seeing that things were going on.

I worked on the pithead for about a year and a half. I was very anxious to get on and made numerous visits to the oversman to see if I could become an underground worker. He always told me that I was too small and too young to go underground.[4] So, taking the law into my own hands, I went up the stair, as we always called it, to see Mr Mackay. His room was upstairs in the Lady Victoria colliery offices. Every time you were notified to go and see Mr Mackay you were

2

told, 'You're goin' up the stair and you're goin' in front o' the Green Table.'

So on this occasion Mr Mackay was very nice to me and told me that he would see the oversman, which was a Mr Mackenzie, in the Dalhousie . section of the pit. Mr Mackenzie approached me the next day on the surface and said he had a job for me underground as a doorboy, a ventilatin' doorkeeper. And I started as a doorboy in the Dalhousie section at the sum of 2/6d.—half-a-crown—a day. I thought I was really in clover, doin' verra well because I had half-a-crown a day.

Now up till then we wis hearin' stories from all our elders about Mr Mungo Mackay, how hard he was, how he wouldn't pay. And you can take it from me that work at that time was verra hard indeed, verra, verra hard indeed. We did not work only six or eight hours a day, we were working ten and twelve hours a day for one day's pay.[5]

During my employment as a doorboy—I was pretty raw at the time—we had oor fireman and my fireman was Jimmy Broon. That wis his name, James Broon. He was one o' the bandsmen wi' the colliery band. So this day Brown and I had an argument. I don't really remember what it was about. But he said to me, he says: 'If you don't behave yoursel',' he says, 'ah'll report ye tae the maister.' Now they always called Mr Mackay the maister, if ye were tae go there. And he said he would report me to the maister. So in my youth and thoughtlessness I said, 'Oh, bugger you and the maister.' So, 'By Joves,' he says, 'you're bein' reported.' So ah wis reported tae the maister and received word that I was to see Mr Mackay the next morning.

'Seein' the maister' was to go up the stair, up in front o' the Green Table. And that meant a lost shift. Ye couldnae go up wi' your muffler on, no, no, that wouldnae do for Mr Mackay. 'Ye've to come up here properly dressed. When you come up to see me come up properly dressed.' Ye werenae properly dressed in Mr Mackay's eyes with a muffler on, to see him. So you had to go home and get changed in your own time. If you were on nightshift ye'd tae come home and be up there at nine o'clock in the mornin'. He never interviewed you durin' your colliery hours. Dayshift, backshift, well, when you were nightshift you come home in the mornin', got your breakfast then went up and saw Mr Mackay. And then ye'd go tae bed, either that or if you drank you went to the Dean Tavern and then you got your dinner and you had the afternoon.[6] And then we used to start nightshift at nine o'clock. But that was the routine. If you were backshift, you'd come in in the mornin'. It didnae matter what time you were there you had tae go on the backshift. It was all on your own time, not in colliery time. Oh, no, no, Mr Mackay wouldnae have that.

And if you were on nightshift you didn't go up the stair then at nine o'clock in the mornin', you know. You were told when to go up the stair. You were down the stair, and there used to be a form that would seat four o' ye. Ye had tae wait yer turn to go up the stair to see Mr Mackay.

Much has been said about Mr Mackay and the Green Table. This was a long table, oh, nine or ten feet long and it wis four feet wide, with mahogany, dark mahogany, ends and the middle of this table had a green baize attached to it. Ah always remember the width o' it because Mr Mackay had his two inkwells on it, one at each side of this green baize, and the inkwells used tae shunt up. And on this green baize there were a wee black book— well, it wisnae very small, if I remember it was a foot in diameter—and this is where all the culprits' names were taken that caused any dissent or disturbance in the colliery. You had to stand in front of the green baize when you were bein' interviewed by Mr Mackay. There were no seat for you. He used to have one chair right outside his office door, and you would sit there. There were never two men allowed to sit outside that office door. You couldn't negotiate wi' one another before you went in to see Mr Mackay. You had to do your negotiatin' downstairs before you went in to see the big boss. That's how he carried on his business. He wis so remarkable that you didn't know really what Mr Mackay was goin' tae say to you when you went before the Green Table.

So when ah wis reported by Jimmy Broon my fireman and had to go up the stair in front o' the Green Table, Mr Mackay told me, he says: 'The fireman's there in place o' me.' There were no deputies when I was a young boy, they were all called fireman. And he says, 'If you haven't got respect for the fireman you have no respect for me,' he says, 'and you'll be up the pit althegither.'

So I had to take it at that, after a good tellin' off about other things. And with my hat in my hand—or my cap rather, because it was a bonnet we wore then—out of the door. That was my first encounter over discipline with Mr Mackay at the Green Table. I'll never forget it.

Time went on and I became a pony driver and my next instance of seeing the Green Table was in a dispute I had with the contractor for not being fast enough bringing in the hutches to the conveyor with my pony. Once again the boy in the big cap, up the stair and into the room to see Mr Mackay. Mr Mackay was sittin' there like the old general behind the green baize table, with the pit policeman sittin' on his right-hand side.

'You sent for me, sir?'

'Yes. What's this you've been doing now?' A complaint had been made about your work and you had to fully explain to Mr Mackay what the complaint was and otherwise.

He was great for discipline. But he wasn't too severe this time. He made me promise that this incident that had happened would never happen again.

When ah wis young you couldnae shift your job. I wis a pony driver. Now tae get away from that job I'd to receive a line from the oversman, signed by the manager, tae make that transfer. If the oversman said he couldnae dispense wi' me tae go tae another job, that wis me stuck. And every job that ye had, either under the oncost—that wis tae the Lothian Coal Company—or a contractor, you had tae get a line o' permission from the man you worked with to be transferred to another job: real dictatorship, real dictatorship.

Jock Darlin' was the name o' ma contractor, and he says, 'Ah'm damned sure ye won't get away tae that job.' I was wantin' tae go to the nightshift. There was more money on the nightshift, which I really needed. So ah signed ma own line. And I got the line: 'You have permission to employ the bearer, Archibald Wilson.' So I takes ma line along tae Mr Darlin', who was very dogmatic, one o' Mr Mackay's henchmen—nothing else, that's all he wis. And ah got it signed by the manager and ah starts on the nightshift next night. Aha! Policeman at the door in the mornin'. I hadnae went tae ma bed that mornin'. 'Mr Mackay wants tae see ye.' So I really thought I was for the high jump, ye know. But after explainin' the position and the conditions o' ma home, which he perfectly knew, because ah wis the breadwinner for mum, ah got away with it. He let me away wi' that exploit. Ah didnae expect it! Ah stayed nightshift for a lot o' years after that.

It was when ah became sixteen ah left the ponies. You had to be over sixteen before you got on to the nightshift. The war was still on at that time. I became what they called a bolter, connecting up the face pans with bolts.

While the stories and complaints went round of the harshness of Mr Mackay, I never came into contact with him for a long period until I went to have a job on my own at what we called brushing. I was road-making underground.

And I took on this road, what we called the top road. There it was: six feet high and eight feet wide, three-and-a-half feet seam. I took that work on contract and it was then, you can believe me, that my trouble did start with Mr Mackay. There were always something wrong wi' your measurement, or the oversman found something wrong with your road—it wasn't big enough or it wasn't to the specification it was supposed to be. And you'd to fight both the oversman and Mr Mackay about every week-end. In these days they used tae tell ye: 'Oh, wait until the next week-end and we'll make it up for you next week.'

Mr Mackay worked every section in the Lady Victoria on a budget. And if these oversmen went and worked this section above the budget price or figure, there was hell to pay. Mr Mackay always—well, let me say, ninety per cent of the time—took the word of his oversman or his fireman. These oversmen that were appointed were much harder, yes, much harder to deal with than Mr Mackay. Because when you wanted to see an oversman you'd to go up to the colliery and perhaps stand at the gate for about an hour until they came up from underground. Now if these oversmen had the suspicion that you were after money you could guarantee they wouldn't come up the pit until five or ten minutes to five, 'cause the offices closed at five o'clock. Of course, the offices were closed before your argument was made over to the oversmen so it was going to be impossible for you that night to get your money. Mr Mackay recognised that, too, and let it go on because it suited his purpose, in accordance to the keepin' of the colliery books.

If you did go to Mr Mackay you had to see both the oversman and the manager, or under-manager, before you got ever enterin' up these stairs tae see Mr Mackay with your grievance. There were many occasions that I went up the stair before seeing the oversman and of course I was chased down

7

again: 'You've no right up here.' And I can remember very well that Mr Mackay was sick of seeing my face for quite a while, being determined, in my thoughts, to get justice.

Mr Mackay always if he didn't believe the workman or didn't understand the report from the fireman, would come down underground into the section himself and really see what was going on. That's one thing I will say about him. He was a justable man. He gave you justice. But to get money out of Mr Mackay was like gettin' blood out o' a stone, I can tell you that. It was very, very hard times when we were young.

I remember another time I was up before the Green Table. I was tree-drawin' in the pit and it was steel props then. Now I always worked in the low seams and at this time it was two-and-a-half feet high. Eventually I lost a prop one night and reported it to the fireman. And the fireman of course had to put me on his sheet and report it. So I was before Mr Mackay again at the Green Table, trying to explain thoroughly how it was impossible for to retrieve this prop. And of course he took the fireman's report and I was fined 7/6d. for losin' that tree—which I thought was a great injustice. It was one o' the occasions really that turned me against Mr Mackay.

When Mr Mackay fined anybody that money was sent to the Edinburgh Royal Infirmary and we always a week afterwards got the wee white slip from the Infirmary with our pay, thanking you for the donation.

His oversmen and his haulage contractors, he had them all drilled the same way. Supposin' you'd went tae the school wi' a mate that worked wi' you for years and years, and he looked for promotion and Mackay saw his potentials and he got an oversman's job or Mackay gave him a contract or some o' the little privileges. He was no longer allowed to co-habit wi' his old pal. He darenae go into the Dean Tavern— that's the public house in Newtongrange—and have his pint there at the bar along with us chaps who he used tae be very friendly with. No. And we used tae get a good laugh at them, ye know. We would be standin' at the bar and would see them openin' the joug bar and lookin' in tae see who was in the jug bar and they wid come in and get this pint, jist like frightened mice. And they wid get this pint and away out the door again. The next time perhaps ye'd see them—they used tae travel round about—they'd go tae Eskbank and ye'd see all these men, maybe five or six o' them, Mungie Mackay's men, all at the bar at Eskbank or further afield. But they were always up before the Green Table if there were the story carried tae Mr Mackay that they had been drinkin' with some o' their old mates. That was Mr Mackay's regime. He was really a dictator, ye know, although he was a gentleman. That's a very contradictory statement, i'n't? But he was.

Now many good things and many bad things have been said about Mr Mackay. One of the good things was that Mr Mackay gave us as miners at that time some o' the best housing conditions in the district or even in Scotland. He was a man who looked after his village. He passed or walked through his village, along with a Mr Terris, the chief surveyor, to see that everything was all right in that village. The situation o' the housing got too big for Mr Terris, and they passed on the lettin' o' the houses to the colliery policeman and it wasnae a great success. But if you didn't keep your garden right you could depend on it that Mr Mackay would either speak to me or to the wife and make sure that I got that garden done and made things tidy.

We had certain cheap rents but that was part of our wages, because at that time our wages was very, very low. And then at other times Mr Mackay could be, aye, well, ye know, very vicious to us. That tree-drawin' incident was an example.

In the 1921 strike, when that come on, well, you know, things were verra bad. We were livin' from hand to mouth. And we had great meetings. So at this meetin' we decided to draw the fires at the colliery. That was the Union's decision—well, it was the men's decision and the men was the Union at that time. We went up to the colliery and we had, oh, well, five or six ringleaders, ye know, blood heated up, and we withdrew the fires at the Lady Victoria colliery. When we was comin' out the yard who's standin' on the main road but Mr Mackay. Now I can say honestly from that date Mr Mackay never forgot the faces of these ringleaders. For, by Jove, after that he gave them a hard time in the pit. The least thing and they were up and gettin' reprimanded.[7]

For at that time we had very little Union lead. The Union leaders was very weak. Our Union—that was the Mid and East Lothian Federation—or ourselves rather, were very weak when it come to bargaining power with the agent. We were always in the same position of not gettin' the proper answers from the negotiation that took place between the colliery agents and our Union representatives. On the whole we weren't really advised or strong enough for to do anything against the private ownership o' the Lothian Coal Company. And at that time if you weren't pleased with one job in a colliery you couldn't really shift to another colliery, because when you did that, or tried to do that, you got word from Mr Mackay that you'd to leave your house.

On one occasion I had a great argument with Mr Mackay about water. I was cuttin' a very wet section at that time. That was down at Carrington and it was on a very steep gradient. Ah says to ma brother, who was ma partner at that time on that coal-cutter, ah says, 'Come on, we're goin' up to see Mr Mackay,' ah says, 'we're goin' tae get some more money here or get another man for tae gie us a hand.' So we went up tae see Mr Mackay and after many arguments, which went from one thing to another, what he would do, what he wouldn't do, well, ah says, 'Mr Mackay,' ah says, 'you can get somebody else for to cut your run.' he says, 'Well, I'll put you out your house.' Ah says, 'Well, you can do what you like.'

So after three weeks of bargaining, back and forward, we'd made nothing of it and he put three men on that coal-cutter. He wouldn't give in to me for another man, or give us a penny more. Ah was cuttin' the coal at 4½d. a ton, that was our tonnage then.

So I got word about a coal-cutter that was goin' in to Arniston colliery. Arniston colliery was owned by another company and Mr Philips was the manager's name there at that time. Ah goes up tae see Mr Philips and he gave me the job right away. He says, 'You're the verra man we're lookin' for. This is a new installation and we're puttin' in this coal-cutter.'[8]

Ah, ha. Before twenty-four hours had passed Mr Mackay had the word down from Arniston that Archie Wilson was startin' on the coal-cutter. The pit policeman came down to my door—Mr Mackay had his own policeman then, the colliery policeman. And every time you saw Mr Mackay at his Green Table the policeman was standin' at one end o' the Table and you were standin' in front o' it, wi' your cap in your hand, sometimes wi' your head bowed.

So up to the Green Table again and Mr Mackay says tae me: 'I understand you've got a job at Arniston?' Ah says, 'Yes, ah'm goin' tae start on Monday.' He says, 'You're not.' He says, 'I'm not allowin' ye tae start at Arniston.' He says, 'There's no house goin' for you up there,' he says, 'in fact, there is no job now either.' He says, 'But I'll tell you what I'll do,' he says, 'I'll let you open up a new section in Dalhousie,' he says. 'You're used to the Dalhousie seams anyway.' Ah says, 'Very good, Mr Mackay,' Ah says, 'What'll the wages be?' He says, 'I'll give you the basic wage.' Ah says, 'Mr Mackay, you won't,' ah says, 'because ah won't start.'

So eventually ah started opening out this section at Dalhousie at 1/6d. above the basic rate, until such time as it was long enough for to go on ton rate.

At that time practically everything was contracted at a price, and beyond that price Mr Mackay wouldn't go. Any difficulties you met you had to work longer hours to finish the job. You had to finish the job, because if you didn't get that run cut within the shift you were there sometimes ten hours— I've seen me twelve hours—workin' and cuttin' that run.

There were no overtime, no overtime, no allowances whatsoever except your bare tonnage. Now these are the things that Mr Mackay could have come and went with, made a little compromise. But Mr Mackay? No, Mr Mackay was a very dominant man in regards to manning and the conditions o' workin' in his colliery.

I will say this about Mr Mackay. In all his instances he was fair but kept you right down to the basic principles o' the agreement that you had signed for, in the makin' o' your roads or the completion o' your work in the pits. He was a hard man to deal with, a very hard man to deal with, a disciplinarian—and that kept you on the proper path. You hadn't the freedom then, you know, as what they have now, 'cause there were always men at the gate, waitin' on your job. These instances prevailed all over Scotland to my knowledge at that time. There were always another man at the gate ready to take over your job.

Mr Mackay was a very remarkable man. He had his finger in every little bit o' business that was takin' place in Newtongrange. In fact, when ah wis younger, he controlled the ambulance, he controlled the telephone—because at that time, if you were in straits whatsoever, ye had tae go up tae the power station, with permission from Mr Mackay, to use the telephone to get in contact with the doctor. Thank God that changed.

But takin' all that into consideration, Mr Mackay must have been a genius for to work the Lady Victoria and the surrounding collieries in the way he did. Before he came to the Lady Victoria he was the manager of Whitehill colliery at Rosewell. Rosewell was under his control then, too.

Mr Mackay had great foresight. He had a trainin' scheme of his own, ye know, in the Lady Victoria, oh, yes. Just after the First World War and durin' that period we had come from what they called common places. A common place was you put your hutch up and you had two men worked here and you had two at the coal and one filled at the boxes and he took it away. And after that they went into the long wall system. They were all on a straight line of fifty fathom walls, main road and ye had top roads. Sometimes ye had a small road in the middle, which was called a dummy road. It wisnae used for anything except for escape purposes. But Mr Mackay realised that with the extension of the workins in the Lady Victoria he'd need more coal men, more face men. What did Mr Mackay do? He got the sons, nephews and cousins of the various coalminers on these faces and put one along with his father, one along with his uncle, or the cousins together, or anybody that was related—but must be related—to receive his trainin' from that man. Now on that relationship ye had no grumbles. Whereas, if the youngster had been with a stranger durin' his trainin' ye would ha' heard all the bloody grumbles o' the day. And that's how he trained his coal men in the seam that ah worked in, that was a two-and-a-half feet seam, in a parrot seam in Dalhousie section. And it was a success. That was the first trainin' scheme that ever ah heard o' and ah became a trainin' officer in the mines later on.

Mr Mackay wasn't jist really a good minin' engineer. Mr Mackay had his finger in every iota in Newtongrange. Even the farm manager: Lingerwood Farm belonged to the Lothian Coal Company, and the manager, Mr Muir, o' that farm, every week had tae bring his books down to Mr Mackay to get them scrutinised. The gas works belonged to the Lothian Coal Company. Mr Bishop, the manager, had to appear practically every mornin' up that stair to make his report in the instances of heat and gas. Colliery managers— we had a manager and an under-manager—saw Mr Mackay every mornin'. The engineers, the blacksmith, the oversman, the gate oversman, the pithead oversman—all had to see Mr Mackay every mornin' and make a report. This was outside the report that was made between four and five every night wi' these same men. So Mr Mackay kept his hand on every pulse that was connected with the minin' industry in New-tongrange. Three pits—Lady Victoria, Easthouses and Lin-gerwood—and a farm: it wasn't an easy job. But he did it.

I remember when the buildin' was going on outside Newtongrange, and the Council complained about the short-age of water. Mr Mackay took it to heart. What did he do? He installed a pump down at the river Esk and pumped the water from the Esk to keep his boilers going so that he would save drinking water for the community. That was one o' the instances that prevailed.

As workmen, we never knew Mr Mackay's salary. If he was well off he never really showed it. He had a family of three sons and two daughters. The sons went tae Daniel Stewart's College in Edinburgh.[9] There were only one o' the sons come into the minin' industry. One went to farmin' and one went to the navy. George, the one that come into the minin' industry, he was a great disappointment to his father.

When Mr Mackay died ah wouldn't say that it caused any great turn up in the village at that time. But the pit was idle that day. The service was in Newbattle Church, at which I was present that day. It was a really remarkable scene to see a funeral of such a man who was spoken about throughout the whole of Scotland for his control of Newtongrange. The pall-bearers at that funeral was contractors. And irrespective of the sadness of the occasion we really did have a great time in the Dean Tavern after the funeral. We certainly did miss his personality in the village for a while after he died. But if it had been possible for Mr Mackay to return today see his village I'm sure he would ha' crawled back into the grave.[10]

From boyhood to manhood I served under Mr Mackay. He was a man who looked into the future, a man that looked after Newtongrange as a village, a man who walked through Newtongrange every week to see that the village was in good condition. And if you'd a complaint about your house that wasn't being attended to, he would see that it was done.

But in his pit dealings he was a hard man to bargain with. Mr Mungo Mackay was both manager and dictator of the Lady Victoria colliery.

ADAM HALDANE

I was always in the minin' industry—fifty-one years frae the time I left the school. But I never was actually doon the pit, except jist an odd shift on certain jobs I was on. Ah was on the surface and ah actually wanted tae go underground—it wid be better wages. Ah had seen auld Bob White in the Lady Victoria. He says, 'Adam, you get a line frae Mungo Mackay and you can start wi' me. You'll get a job wi' me any time you want.' Ah wis on Easthooses pitheid at this time. But ah couldnae get a line frae Mungo Mackay tae go doon the pit. And ah lived tae bless the day that he never allowed me tae go doon the pit, because it wisnae a good job, neither for men nor management, minin'.

Ah wis born in Newtongrange in September 1903. Ma father wisnae a miner either, because he wis on the pumps actually. He worked at the Bryans—that wis a real auld pit—when ah wis a youngster.[11] But he had had a bad illness when ah wis a bairn and he had tae give up minin' and went on tae other work. Then he was what they ca' a deputy nowadays, and in latter years he was a kind o' foreman doon the pit.

Possibly ma father would start work before he was fourteen. He wis born about 1875 in Auld Pentland, in the Loanhead area. He married ma mother, who was a Lasswade woman, and they shifted from there ower tae Whitehill. That would be when he would start in the Bryans.

Whitehill wis jist on the Pathhead road, jist above Easthooses roadend. My oldest brother was born in Whitehill.

The rest o' us—four sons and four daughters—were a' born in Newtongrange.

Ma father's father was in the minin' industry a' his life as well: Auld Bob. He wis a wee man, he widnae be much over five feet. His wife was a big woman.

I suppose that some o' ma forebears would probably be the women that brocht the coal up on their backs. There wis a place, ye know, at Easthouses where they yaised tae bring the coal up on their backs. But I cannae remember ma grandfather Auld Bob sayin' much about his forebears in the pits.[12] Ye see, I didnae have an awful lot to dae wi' ma grandfather until ma granny died. When she died we came down frae the wee houses in Abbeyland into ma grandfather's house tae look after him. His hoose was bigger, it wis double-storey. There wis two bedrooms up the stair, and fairly big rooms they were tae. They could sleep four or five in them. And then there wis aye a bed in the livin' room—ma parents slept there. And ma grandfaither had the other room doon the stair for hissel'. These downstair rooms were flagstane flairs. Ah can mind they were covered wi' linoleum, but ye could see the mark o' every brick through the linoleum.

You've heard o' the tied houses on the agricultural side. But it wis jist the same in the pits. Ye wis virtual serfs. Even when ah wis married first ye were serfs. It wis a case o' as long as ye did and said what they wanted ye to do and say ye wis a'right. But if ye put a step wrong it wis a case o' 'Get your sticks on the lorry and flit.' Ye wis tied tae the house. And of course Mungo Mackay knew these things! He could put the boot in efter ye wis a married man and had a wife and a faimly.

Ah'm no' gaun tae say that he ever did very much wi' me, because although I wis a kind o' renegade now and again, I aye kind o' stuck to the rules. Ye had tae if ye had ony respect for yer ain wife and faimly, yer ain hame and that. Ye had tae. Ye had tae toe the line.

Well, ah wis fourteen in September 1917. Ye had tae go to the school of course until the Christmas holidays. And I wis runnin' aboot loose for a few weeks. I think I wid start work aboot January 1918. Ah started tae work then at Easthooses mine, on the pithead.

My first run-in with Mungo Mackay was when I was sixteen years of age. Wir daily job at that time on the pithead was from ten minutes to six in the mornin' until four in the afternoon, or something after four. But oo wis always expected tae stay until aboot six o'clock at night, to do a bit overtime. And ah got a wee bit fed up wi' this and ah had a talk wi' some o' the other boys. 'Ach, we'll hae a nicht off now and again.'

So this got back to Mungo Mackay's ears. And, oh, he took me to task aboot this. Ah wis accused then o' bein' the leader o' a strike at sixteen years o' age! He telt me that if ah wis needed at the pit I wid be there. Ah says, 'Look, Mr Mackay,' ah says, 'are you tellin' me that if I bocht a ticket that's five bob tae go tae a dance or somethin' and ah'm wanted tae stey on here,' ah says, 'ah have tae loss that five bob tae get half-a-croon for workin' here?' Ah says, 'It'll never happen.' It feenished up at the hinder end, ah says: 'Look,' ah says, 'if ah have nothin' better tae dae ah'll be here. But,' ah says, 'if ah have somethin' better tae dae I'm no' gaun tae be here.' That wis that!

That wis the way, ah think, ah got off on the wrong foot wi' Mungo Mackay. Him and I never saw eye to eye on very many things. Of course the biggest trouble was that ah couldnae be a yes-man. If ah thocht he wis wrong I'd tell him he wis wrong.

Ah wis at Easthooses for eight or nine years then ah came tae the central workshops at the Lady Victoria. Ah wis there for a long time, on quite a number o' jobs—foreman, and things like that. Then ah went back tae Easthooses, jist at the beginnin' o' the Second World War. I wis on loco-drivin'. Then I went on to what they cried the rope haulage at Lady Victoria. Then ah wis sent tae Easthouses, tae the windin' o' the men and ah wis there tae the end o' the chapter as far as ah wis concerned. I retired in September 1968 and Easthooses wis closed in October the following year. I used tae often say tae ma mates, 'Well, this pit's went a long time withoot Mungo Mackay. I dinnae think it'll gaun very long withoot me!'

But Mungo Mackay, he was a real martinet. He was also a great organiser. When they started what they called long wall working they had what they called pan runs. Now these pans, they bought them in frae a manufacturer first. But after that the Lothian Coal Company made them themselves. Mungo Mackay pinched everybody's patents and they made them up in the central workshops. They created great big presses for making these pans. Each length would be six feet and they'd be maybe fifteen or eighteen inches at the top, tapered slightly in. And there was a metal chain run along these pans for conveyin' the coal to their outlet. They manufactured a' these themselves up in the central workshops. There were a lot o' good tradesmen there. It used tae be said that any chap that served his time wi' the Lothian Coal Company could get a job anywhere if he was a decent tradesman at all, because we turned oot grand tradesmen. Ye'd a great workshop up there and we really had a lot o' good practical men.

They had a great set-up at Newbattle in these days. The pits there in my earliest recollections o' them were Lingerwood, Bryans, Lady Victoria, Easthouses mine, and there was a wee place they called Vexem. I don't know whether Vexem got that nickname because it had vexed somebody. I think they were goin' tae sink a pit there and it didnae turn oot successful. They discovered some geological trouble or something. So they went a wee bit further north to Easthouses and sunk a mine there. And they put in two engines at Vexem, wi' ropes that went down from there into Easthouses mine, and these engines drew the coal up to the Easthouses mine. But Vexem was a name that Mungo Mackay jist widnae tolerate. He wid never have it called the Vexem. He widnae have nane o' thae names. Tae him it wis 'Bryans' extension'.

As far as Mungo Mackay's minin' engineering was concerned, ye've heard tell o' pit bottoms? Now ah suppose your idea o' a pit bottom would be ye got doon in the cage and ye went away along a low road. That didnae exist in the Lady Victoria. The pitbottom there would be aboot as big as Newtongrange Picture Hoose. Great big high walls, and all whitewashed. It wis a beautiful place, actually, tae be underground. All the roadways were very, very well maintained. Although ah never worked in it, I know a' the outs and ins o' the industry. The pits were very, very well maintained. Ah believe that Mungo Mackay—if he'd been a younger man wi' the advent o' nationalisation—he'd really been one o' the big noises in the industry, because he really was a first class minin' engineer. I don't think there wis his equal in this country. But unfortunately it wis too late for him.

He was a great economist as well. There wis never ever anythin' allowed tae waste. If he was walkin' along and somebody wis there wi' him and they saw a bolt lyin' on the ground they were telt tae pick it up. It wis put away in scrap, sold for scrap metal. He wasted nothing that man, nothing ever was wasted.

In hindsight Mungo Mackay had a lot goin' for him. He had a lot o' good things aboot him. There wis another thing that always stuck wi' me that I rather admired the man for. Well, it wis the same in thae days as what it is now: ye had folk that were kind o' mentally retarded and some o' them wis lame, crippled, and things like that. But Mungo Mackay found a job for them. If they were able to go and do anythin'

20

they got a job. Ah cannae remember very many folk bein' idle.

There were yin, they ca'ed him Daft Jimmy Samuel. He wis a man but he wid have the intelligence o' a wee boy. He used tae get bad spells o' almost madness at the job he was on, on the pickin' tables. The pickin' tables was when the coal come up the pit. It was a' done at the Lady Victoria. A' the coal come doon tae the Lady Victoria. The hutches came from Easthouses and from Lingerwood and they were a' tipped on the tumblers—the tippin' machine—on tae a scree, like a screen. And a' the dross was screened out there. Then ye had the pickin' tables. They would be four feet wide, and there wis bars, an endless belt, and there wis people there pickin' a' the stones oot, cleanin' the whole. The sortin' tables, they called them some places. There wis a lot o' coal went ower that place in a day, because the Lady Victoria in ma heyday could be daein' 2,000 to 2,500 tons a day on the dayshift. Then ye had another 800 or 900 tons comin' in frae Easthouses and frae Lingerwood. Then a' the dross o' course went to the washin' machine and was washed there as well.

Well, Daft Jimmy Samuel got a job on the pickin' tables jist the same. I remember yince when I was a kind o' foreman at the pickin' tables and Daft Jimmy wis in such a state. This day another foreman along wi' me actually had a rope lying aside tae tie him up in case he got stupeless a'thegither. He could ha' gotten violent. He wid tell ye what he got violent aboot but I'll no' tell ye here.

At Easthouses there wis a young lad that wis on the engines along wi' me. He wasnae very badly disabled but when he was young he had had bovine tuberculosis in one o' his knees. He was pretty lame. But that chap had a job tae. And I knew quite a lot o' them there. Well, there wis John Rutherford, he wis a heid man in the miners' union. He had a leg off but he always worked in the pits. John wisnae a full-time union official, oh, no. In his later years he worked as what ye ca'ed a shover-on. He wis pushin' the loaded hutches off. And there was old John Hamilton that was in the same position. Pinny Hamilton they called him, because he had a pin leg. He was in what they called the justice box.

The justice box was where the coal come up the pit it was weighed in the hutches. Ye had two men in the justice box. Ye had the Lothian Coal Company's man and ye had the justice man. The justice man was a union employee and wis seein' that the men got their right weight. That was yin thing that Mungo Mackay would never hear—he would never hear ye ca' it the justice box! It wis like makin' a reflection on the Lothian Coal Company, that there had tae be somebody to see that the men got justice. He called it the weigh office, the weigh office. He was a stickler for that.

Ah had lots o' experiences wi' Mungo Mackay and, as ah say, ah didnae get on very well wi' him. But he wis a fair man in certain weys and he wis a good man in certain weys, too.

Mungo Mackay's salary we never knew. He had mair than 5/10d. a day, ye can take ma word for that. He had a big job, because he was the Lothian Coal Company's agent. He had three pits that he had tae work wi'. In fact, there wis a wee while that he wid hae four, because I think the Bryans was still goin' when Easthooses started. And, as ah say, there wis another place they cried Vexem where they were tryin' tae produce coal.

Newtongrange wis a wonderful village in Mungo Mackay's times, ye know. When ah think back on it I often say yet, 'You know, they were happy days,' because yer neighbours were a' the same as you. There wis nane o' ye had anything. But ye wis aye prepared tae share everything wi' a neebour. It wis a happy life, well, they used tae say folk wis content in thae days. But I used tae say folk had tae be content, because there were nothin' else for it. Ye had tae be content wi' what ye had.

But it was a model village in Mackay's time, because he saw that it wis kept a model village. That wis pairt o' your missive for your house. Ye had tae keep yer garden cultivated and everythin'. If there wis onybody that didnae keep it cultivated he yaist tae send men doon and cultivate it for them and take it off their pey! That wis the kind o' life it wis in Newtongrange.

There wis one thing that ah didnae like aboot Mungo Mackay. He interfered far too much wi' folks' private life, if ye know what ah mean. He knew a' that wis gaun on. He knew everythin' aboot your life, both private and public, and he could always use that against ee if it wis possible. If onybody had created a kind o' misdemeanour—nothin' at a' tae dae wi' the pit—oot in the village, he wid have them up at the Green Table aboot it. And he wid fine them. If he wis finin' them five bob or ten bob, they got a wee slip o' paper in their pey box, thankin' them for their donation that had been sent tae the Royal Infirmary! Oh, right enough, the Lothian Coal Company didnae steal ony o' thae fines. They were sent away tae charitable institutions. I think the Royal Infirmary got most o' them.

He found oot aboot the private lives o' the miners because he had the greatest o' espionage systems. It wis almost like the KGB in Russia. He was well informed. He knew everythin' that was gaun on. He knew the day that ye wis married and the day that ye had a faimly. And, as ah say, if ye wis married and had a house and a family he could put the boot in. Ye had tae dae whatever ee wis telt or it wis, 'Get your sticks on the lorry and get out.'

He had spies, oh, by Jove, aye. Ah suppose a lot o' them would be known but ah couldnae mention any o' their names. But ye know there wis a lot o' his oversmen and a' these kind o' men who took a' the stories up. In fact, ah could tell ee yin thing in particular aboot him. It wis a' in much later days, it wisnae very long before Mungo's regime came to an end. Ah wis doin' a kind o' foreman's job up aboot the Lady Victoria pithead at the time. Ah happened tae go intae the enquiry office jist inside the gate yonder for somethin' that night, and the phone rung when ah wis there. It wis Mungo Mackay askin' if John MacDonald was there. That wis the chap that wis in charge o' the Lady Victoria end o' the pithead. Ah wis in charge o' the Easthouses and Lingerwood end. Wullie Paxton answered the phone and he says tae Mungo: 'Ah'm afraid that John is away home. But,' he says, 'Adam Haldane's here, if he wid be any use tae ye.' 'Send him up.' So up ah went. And Mungo Mackay asked me: was ah aware that the pit had been held up for two minutes on the surface yesterday? What was wrong? 'Well,' ah says, 'it's no' ma pairt o' the pitheid but,' ah says, 'ah can tell ee this much,' ah says, 'the pitheid had never held the pit up for two minutes yesterday.' He was sittin' with the tachograph—you know the thing they've got in the motor lorries nowadays? Well, they had a tachograph on the windin' engine and everythin' wis a' recorded there. This wis where he found out that the pit had been held up for two minutes, waitin' on the signal from the pithead. 'Mr Mackay,' ah says, 'would ee look at the date on that tachograph? Because,' ah says, 'the pit didnae stand for two minutes yesterday,' ah says. 'It wis the day before!' Oh, that did it! He wis hammerin' the table efter that.

Then he says tae me, 'In any case,' he says, 'ye never come up here and tell me anythin'.' So ah looked at him and ah says: 'Mr Mackay,' ah says, 'when you appointed me tae take charge o' that particular section o' the pithead,' ah says, 'ah understood that that would take some o' the worries o' that section off o' you and land them on me. And,' ah says, 'if ah had nothin' tae complain aboot in that section,' ah says, 'ah have no intention o' comin' here tae see you. If ah'm in ony trouble and need ony advice or help,' ah says, 'ah'll come ower. But otherwise ah have nae intention o' comin' ower. If ye're expectin' me tae come up and tell ye every wee bit tittle tattle ah hear, then,' ah says, 'ah'm no' gaun tae be very long in a job.' And neither ah wis, because ah widnae gaun up and tell him everythin'.

But that wis the kind o' wey he got his information, ye see. It wis expected o' certain men that if they were gaun tae keep their jobs and keep sweet wi' Mungo Mackay they wid go up and tell him a' the stories, baith in the public side and in the pit side. He expected that o' ee.

A chap that ah knew in Newtongrange that went away tae Perth in Australia came home once and was tellin' me an experience that he had wi' Mungo Mackay. It wis at the Pend, a wee tunnel over which the mineral railway ran. It wis supported by big heavy girders and oo used tae go in and swing on these girders. Oo used tae skin the cat on them. And this laddie had been seen skinnin' the cat on the girders this day when Mungo Mackay was passin' in his gig. He said tae the man that wis drivin': 'Get a hold o' these boys.' And somebody said tae this chap—George White his name wis— 'Watch and no' get catched, for, mind, if he catches ye, yer faither'll get the seck.' That wis the kind o' regime that we lived in in these days.

Another thing, Mungo Mackay was the First Master o' the Masonic Lodge in Newtongrange. His portrait used tae be in the Lodge but for a long time it was missin'. And while I was yin that never got on very weel wi' him, ah said, 'Now that portrait should be there and it should be up where it can be seen.' And I insisted on this until at last I got his portrait back up in the Lodge room. Because irrespective of what he may have been to me or to anybody else he was the first Master o' the Lodge and as such must be respected. So his portrait's still in the Lodge room yet.

But I don't think bein' a member o' the Masonic craft had

very much influence as far as gettin' jobs wi' the Lothian Coal Company went. Merit, merit, ah think, was the main thing. Mungo Mackay was in the Masonic craft when he came frae Auchinleck in Ayrshire tae the Lothian Coal Company. And possibly that was the reason a' his best friends were Masons, because he was the Master and they all jined the Lodge in Newtongrange. All his foremen were Ayrshire men. Well, it maybe wouldnae be right tae say they were a' Ayrshire men. But they were a' Clydesiders. The technicians on the Clyde were really first-class men. I think that wis mair the reason they were doing mechanical jobs and things like that wi' the Lothian Coal Company.

I think the miners' trade union officials were very much in Mungo Mackay's pocket, tae, because they had tae be. When ah started work first it wid be the Mid and East Lothian Miners' Union ah wis in. The men used tae come roond for yer contribution aye. They came roond the hooses. I mind there were yin auld yin frae Easthooses, Tommy Campbell they cried him. He aye had a pocketfae o' yon wee aromatic sweeties. And aye when he cam in the hoose for the union dues there were twa or three o' thae sweeties left on the dresser for the bairns.

The union wid be a pit branch at that time. It wid incorporate a' these pits, Lingerwood, Lady Victoria and Easthooses. They would be a' in the yin branch, as wid be the auld Bryans earlier than that. But they would hae their ain branch ower there again at Rosewell. It wis the same ower there—ye had mair than one pit ower there. Ye had Polton and Rosewell.

Ah remember our union man John Rutherford very well. Ah steyed next door tae him for years and years. Ah got on very well wi' John. Oh he wis a fair good man. He was a Newtongrange man. He wis in Newtongrange a' ma life onyway. Aye, he wis a fair-sized man, John, and walked very well, too, wi' the pin leg o' course they had in thae days. In later years he had yin o' the mair modern artificial legs. He wid be thirty or thirty-five year aulder than me. Oh, he was a fair good man but, as ah say, in these days they couldnae be very militant.

Efter the 1914–18 War, right enough, when ah wis first at work, you begun tae see the beginnins o' trade unionism takin' a wee bit stronger hold. There wis quite a few chaps in Newtongrange that died in the War. Ma eldest brother Bob and another chap Jimmy Birrell they were wantin', I suppose, tae get off intae the airmy so they would still be earnin' money tae come intae the hoose tae bring up the rest o' us. They wid be excused military duty because they were workin' in the pit, ye see. But ye had tae get a recommendation frae yer boss tae jine up. And I dinnae ken how it came aboot but Mungo Mackay had said somethin' that he didnae like, somethin' aboot no' tae come crawlin' tae him. 'Crawlin' tae you?', says ma brother Bob, 'I widnae crawl tae you nor tae nae other body.' He says, 'Ah'll gaun away and join the navy the morn.' And he went away in the mornin' and jined the navy. The two o' them, Jimmy Birrell and him, went.

Then ah remember ma father and I think two o' his brothers and two other chaps went intae Edinburgh frae Newtongrange tae be attested under the Derby Scheme, to see if they would be fit for foreign service.[13] It wis a Sunday they went, and when they come back I asked ma faither how he'd got on. 'Oh,' he says, 'we din no' sae bad,' he says. 'They got twa and a half sojers oot o' the five o' us.' That wis two that wis fit for foreign service, one that wis fit for home service only, and two that wis no use at all for service!

There wis this story ah heard aboot some Newtongrange chaps that wis away in the First World War. They came back after it tae get their jobs, of course. But Mungo Mackay wisnae verra keen tae gie them their jobs. He said to them:

'You wis the boys that wis tippin' the water butts.' A lot o' folk had big water barrels at the back o' the house and these chaps had been gaun roond, ye know, before they'd gone tae the War. It wisnae vandalism, it wis high spirits, tippin' the water butts. But that wis enough: they werenae gaun tae get a job at the pit because they had been tippin' the water butts.

Now there were other two or three o' these chaps. Gene Burnett was yin o' them, and another yin was Rodgers. They had been artillerymen durin' the War and were well acquainted wi' workin' wi' horses. They kent that Mungo Mackay used tae gaun ower tae Lasswade on a certain nicht in the week wi' the powny and trap, the gig, visitin' somebody there. And these lads made up their mind that they would meet Mungo comin' frae his safari at Lasswade and gie him a hard hurl hame. So they waylaid him yin o' the nichts, took over the reins o' the horse, and gave him one hell of a hard hurl hame tae Lingerwood House, Newtongrange. But they were sent for and they got their jobs back again.

Well, Mungo Mackay died in 1939. I mind it wis a big funeral. I wis at the funeral. There wis an awful lot o' folk there. Ah'm no' sure if it wid be oot o' respect or gled tae see him away! Oh, although I didnae get on wi' the man, ye know, well, oo wis kind o' brocht up that way, tae hae respect for yer elders.

Efter the 1939–45 War, when nationalisation did come in there was a terrible difference in the minin' industry. Ah could gie ye a couple o' instances, but yin wis there wis a foreman in the engineering shop o' the Lothian Coal Company—Jim Paxton. Now Jim Paxton was a very serious-faced man, very sour-faced man, actually. But from the day that nationalisation come in that man was a different man althegither. He had been a man that wid hardly speak tae anybody. This is the kind o' regime, ye see, that they lived under wi' Mungo Mackay and the Lothian Coal Company. If ye wis gaun tae be a foreman or an official o' any kind under the Lothian Coal Company ye had tae be a pure so-and-so. It bred that in ee. Ye had tae be that wey if ye was gaun tae keep a job. Ye had tae screw yer men doon if ee was gaun tae keep a job. But wi' nationalisation there wis a' the difference in the world.

JAMES 'TREACLE' MOFFAT

I first went down the Lady Victoria pit in 1916. Mr Mackay was the general manager there and o' Lingerwood, Easthouses and Whitehill at that time. He wis a bad man and he wis a guid man. Ah mean, he was a bad man, he wisnae feared tae tell ye if ye done onythin' wrong: 'Ah'll put ye out the house.' Ye had tae dae what ye wis telt—or else.

His heid man as manager o' the Lady Victoria was Willie Carson and the under-manager wis Peter Dixon. And they telt ye, 'Ye'll do what ye're told—or else.' An' he says to me one day, 'Ye'll do what ye're told or ah'll put ye out your house.' So ah says, 'Well, ye'll just have to put ez out the house.' Ah says, 'Ah've a good home tae go tae.' 'Aye,' he says, 'if ye gane back to yer faither and mither we'll pit them out the house too.' Ah wis married. Ah steyed away up at the top o' Lingerwood Road at the time.

Ah can remember miners that were actually pit oot their hoose by Mungo Mackay. There were Bobby Gordon an' George Letham. Ah dinnae ken what they'd done. Ah jist ken they were pit oot their hoose and they went to Arniston.

If ye didnae dae yer garden they sent a man to do the garden and there were £2 kept of your pey for to pay for him. But that never happened to me or to any miner that ah kent.

Mungo Mackay was a tall man. He wis friendly, he wisnae bad. He jist went doon through the village wi' a powny and trap and had a run roond aboot and back intae the house. Ah don't think Mr Mackay was what ye'd call a visitor. And ah think he always went to Cockpen Church on a Sunday mornin'. Ah think he wis an elder there.

And he got the Freemasons started doon at the Newbattle Lodge there. He started up the pipe band tae. He maistly a' started a' thae things.

Mungo Mackay lived up there—he had a big hoose—at the pit. If he came back and seen his big hoose, his braw big hoose, made intae a car park up there, by Jove, he wid go his miles. Aye, he'd be sayin', 'Ye never asked ma permission to knock it doon.'[14]

He had two sons. And there were yin, he was a great lad. He wid say, 'Ah'm late. Ah'll hae tae take the car.' The squire says to him, 'Ye'll get no car, take the bus.' Ah think that was young George Mackay.

Jist aboot the time o' the First World War a lot o' Poles came tae Newtongrange.[15] In the Stane Block, that's where a lot o' the Poles came to first, to the Stane Block. Well, they cried it the Pole Barracks. There were two Poles bid thegither, Mitchell and Paterson, and they had a lot o' lodgers. They were a' Poles and they used to gin oot in the back gairden and play at cairds. An' a row would start. They used to gin ower and tear off palin' stabs and batter yin another wi' the palin' stabs. An' Mungo Mackay wid send workmen doon the next day to pit up a new palin'. And he telt them, he says: 'Every time ye tear the palin' doon, ah'll send workmen doon for the new palin'. But,' he says, 'you'll pay for it. An',' he says, 'you'll pay for the wood.' So there werena so much fightin' efter that.

Och, ah've seen them—the twa polismen in Nitten at the time was big Wull Leadin'ham an' big Wull Bourland—when a fight started yin day an' somebody must have telt them. When the twa polismen came merchin' up the road and cut in tae where ye gaun in tae the baths, the Poles must ha' seen the polismen comin' and they lifted their jaickets and away and landed away doon in the Sticky Wid. That wis before the First World War, ah think ah wis jist at the school at the time.

I had tae gaun up tae the Green Table. Ye had tae gaun up the stair to see him. Ah had got a job on the pony-drivin' at the Lady Victoria and ma powny ran away. When oo went up tae the splint mine the oversman, Jimmy Long, was stan'in' wi' the powny. He says, 'What's the powny daein' up here itsel'?' Ah says, 'It run away.' It could run harder than me. 'Aw? Ye'll have to see Mr Mackay aboot that.' So ah was sent for. They put a line on your token: 'Gaun up and see Mr Mackay at four o'clock.' An' when ah went up he says, 'What have you been doin'?' And ah says, 'Nothin' that ah ken o'.' So he says, 'You must have been daein' somethin'.' Ah says, 'It must be about ma powny runnin' away.' 'Aye,' he says, 'that's right.' So oo had a wee bit blether back and forrit and he says, 'Aye, jist tae learn ye a lesson,' he says, 'oo'll fine ye ten bob but ye'll get it back in three month on your good behaviour.' So ah wis good behaviour for the next three month and ah got back ma ten bob.

If there were a fight in the Dean the night he knew tomorrow mornin'. His spies were jist a' folk that went aboot him, them that got a contract for bein' an informant. And the pit polisman was aye runnin' roond lookin' for onything that wis troublesome and he jist went right up and telt him.

When Mungo Mackay died ah didnae attend his funeral. The road was a' lined doon the street, right doon to below the Dean Tavern. Well, everybody had the same view o' him, that he was a kind o' bad man an' he was a kind o' guid man at times. If ye went up tae see him, if he sent for ye to gin up, he wid argue wi' ye an' he wid grant ye your side o' the story if he thocht ye wis right. So ah think he wis quite fair in that wey.

JOHN TELFER

Ah came to Lingerwood in June 1918 and ah started on the farm there, jist a boy o' fourteen. The farm belonged to the Marquis o' Lothian. It was rented by the Lothian Coal Company frae the Marquiss o' Lothian and they kept it up till the Coal Board took over and then they gave it up.

The way the Lothian Coal Company took the farm was to feed the pit ponies. Well, when ah came to Lingerwood ah think there would be close on eighty ponies in the Lady Victoria. There werenae many in Lingerwood pit—ah think there would jist be about two or three.

The meat for the ponies was a' made up here at Lingerwood Farm. They had a hay-cutter, a big wheel with two blades which cut the hay; and then in the top loft—there were three lofts—the oats and the bran and the maize came down into a box and the hay was blewn up and it was a' mixed wi' a mixer and come down. The women that was workin' on the farm bagged it and it was tied of course and stored for the ponies.

But that's the way they kept the farm on, for the sake o' the ponies. And jist by degrees Mr Mackay got a' the ponies out o' the pit. He jist pit in what they ca'ed mane-and-tails in these days, ye ken: the rope run in wi' the weight o' the empty bogie and o' course the wee engine pulled it out. He did that through the whole pit and eventually a' the ponies was dissolved.

Ah worked on the farm wi' the ladies, the girls. There were

only seven women on the farm because they had to make the chop for the ponies, ye see. We worked in the fields after. On a wet day ye'd come in and make chop for the ponies.

Ah used to feed the sheep for Mr Muir, that was the farm manager. He used to buy hogs at St Boswells and we fed them on the turnips. After that ah got the odd horse to drive. Ah drove it for aboot a couple o' year and then there were one o' the ploughmen retired and ah had a pair o' horse after that. And here the grieve left. He gave up because there were something wrong. Ah says to Mr Muir, the auld manager, ah says, 'Mr Muir, could ah no' get the grieve's job?' He says, 'Div ye think ye can dae it, Johnny?' Ah says, 'There's nothin' tae hinder me.' He says, 'Can you stack?' Ah says, 'Ah cannae stack but ah've had a bit try.' So, however, he says, 'Fair enough,' he says. So ah got on to be grieve for the old man, and I used to be very kind to him. Ah seen things wis right.

Well, the first time ah came in contact wi' Mungo Mackay, the old farm manager Mr Muir wasnae in very good shape and ah wis daein' his books and everything. And ah wis goin' down what they ca'ed the bankin' side towards the pit offices and Mungo Mackay had passed me. So the nixt day ah wis in seein' him he says, 'Telfer,' he says, 'wis that you that ah saw comin' down there with the books?' Ah says, 'Yes, sir.' He says, 'Have you been doin' the books?' 'Yes,' ah says, 'ah've been doin' them for Mr Muir,' ah says, 'all the time he's been ill.'

Old Mr Muir died in 1936. So ah gaed down to see Mungo Mackay an' he says tae me: 'We'll have a look at the job,' he says, 'we'll see.' So him an' a chap came—I think it was their lawyer—and went round the farm wi' me and oo had a look at the fields an' things. The chap that was wi' him had seemed to ken something aboot agriculture because he says, 'It's been kept in very good order.' So the next day ah went down, Mr Mackay says, 'Oo havenae decided yet, Mr Telfer, but tomorrow . . .', he says. So ah became the farm manager in 1936.

When ah got the job Mr Mackay says, 'Telfer,' he says, 'you'll get the same as what Mr Muir got.' Oo didnae pay no rent or anything, we had a free house, and oo had free coal and a wage forbye. And he was verra kind tae me. He always appreciated anything ah told him, ye ken. And he used often tae say, 'How's the farm goin' on?' And that was a' there wis to it. But otherwise he was a perfect gentleman tae me. Ah couldnae say anything.

Well, Mr Mackay was very well liked in Newtongrange. He was strict but he was good. And, mind ye, if anybody was off ill they got their coals jist the same. They wid only pey them up maybe so much at a time, if they had been off several weeks. He was very good that way. And the rents wisnae big.

He was very prone aboot the gardens. If people didnae do their gardens, he was at them, and there werenae a dirty garden in the village, ah can assure ye o' that. He told them, he jist told them if they had to get it done and it wis done. At that time, you know, the old miner was a block that look-ed efter his garden. They used tae have a flower show, they used to have a leek show and various other things. Mr Mackay himsel' didnae act as the judge at these shows. There were aye men appointed—gardeners frae various places. I knew one chap, he came frae Rosslynlee, and various others, maybe frae Dobbie's.[16] And they judged the gardens. And then there were a prize for the best kept garden. A chap Melrose that stayed down jist at the top of Lingerwood Road, he had a perfect garden. And he always won the first prize for the best-kept garden. The gardens in Newtongrange was perfectly kept.

Ah think Mr Mackay was perfect for the village because he kept it in order. At that time he had painters, he had plumbers, he had joiners and slaters that maintained the village the whole time. If there were slates off they jist come up and seen Mr Terris, which was the clerk o' works, and he gave the plumber or the bricklayer or whatever a line, and the chap jist got his material and went off and done the job.

Mr Mackay hadnae a motor car at this time, it wis jist a pony and trap and Mr Rutherford was the man that look-ed after it. The pony was kept at the farm. Mr Rutherford was on call all the time, an' if Mr Mackay was goin' tae East-houses or various places he had to be on the dot. Mr Mackay whiles had a bit drive up and down the village, and he was verra good at pickin' up an old miner in aside him, and maybe takin' him oot to Easthouses to get a bit crack wi' him. That was the type o' man he wis.

There were an old chap by the name o' Rob Darling had been up seein' Mr Mackay about something. And Mr Mackay says to him, 'Darling,' he says, 'ye're a real darling.' He says, 'Mr Mackay,' he says, 'ye're the real Mackay.'

WILLIAM TAYLOR

I stay in Eighth Street, Newtongrange, and I've been in Eighth Street for fifty-odd years. I started work as a miner in the Lady Victoria. Ah wis a pony driver, ah wis a chalker, ah wis a shover-upper, ah wis a conveyorman, ah wis everything. And when the seven-hour day started—ah think it wis the seven-hour day—they put fillers along wi' the facemen in Dalhousie section o' the pit, and ah wis one o' the fillers because ma faither was a faceman, ye see.

It wis about three month after that, ah think, when there were no more fillers—'Take a face line job.' And ah wis workin' immediately below ma faither, until ah got ma hand broken. Ah got ma hand broken—ah think it wis 1921—wi' a fa'ed roof, well, it wis lack o' concentration, stupidity. Anyway, ah decided that ah wanted tae be better off than oncost, because the oncost wage was 6/3d. and that wisnae suitable for me, because there were only yin pey comin' into the hoose—ma faither's—and there were five below me. And ma pey was verra, verra small at 6/3d.

So ah went up tae Arniston, tae Stobhill, and ah got in touch wi' a man called Andrew Howie. He was a great teacher for firemen or anything. And he says, 'You're no' wantin' tae be a fireman.' 'No,' ah says, 'ah don't think so anyway. No,' ah says, 'ah want tae get up, I have tae get up. I need money.'

So wi' me always stayin' along or bein' sent along wi' the electrician in Dalhousie section, ah got experience off o' them. Ah kent how tae dae the cables and a' the rest o' it. So yin o' the electricians, Andrew Garrett, says, 'Ye'll gaun and see John Samuel, that's the heid electrician. Gaun up and see him the day, and ye've tae gaun hame and get dressed,' he says, 'because he thinks that ye'll have tae go and see Mr Mackay.' 'Oh.'

So ah got hame and ah got washed. Now it wis a crime in ma hoose if ah got washed first. There were only twa o' us in the pit, ma faither and me, but ye had nae richt tae get washed first. Ee was second on the list for gettin' washed. And ah used tae lie doon in the bath and fa' asleep. Anyway, ah gets a' washed and cleaned. Ma mother says, 'Where are ee gaun?' Ah says, 'Ah'm gaun up tae the office.' 'Ah, but ye're sharely gettin' dressed for't?' 'Well,' ah says, 'ah wis telt tae be kind o' respectable.' 'Oh, aye,' she says, 'put on your second suit.' So ah gins ben and pits the second suit on and comes oot the door when ma faither wis coming in.

'Where are ee gaun?' he says. Ah says, 'Ah'm gaun up tae see John Samuel,' ah says. 'They tell me ah'm tae get a job frae him,' and ah says, 'ah might hae tae gaun up and see Mackay.' 'Ah, that's a different game,' he says. 'Have ye spoken tae him, have ye seen him?' 'No, but,' ah says, 'ah've seen him on the wa', and ah mind o' him shoutin' tae auld Jock Tait aboot'—what wis they said? Oh, aye, Jock wis the only man that ever I heard ca'in' him Mungie. Jock Tait frae the raw at Gowkshill, the only man that could ca' him Mungie Bill. That's what he said tae him. He said, 'Ye're gaun ower thae pans, Mungie, jist like a muckle coo.' He wis a plooman, of course, Jock, he wis in the plooman trade onyway. 'Like a muckle coo,' he says. Ah, that didnae please Mungie. So at the end o' the week there wis 3/6d. off o' Jock Tait for puttin' a large sleeper up on top o' a single tree. Ye daurnae use a large sleeper. Ye use a lid. And that cured that bit. 'Aye,' he said, 'ah'll nae be cairryin' messages.' Jock apparently had cairried love notes between Mungie Mackay and his girlfriend, back and forrit, and Jock had cairried thae notes.

So anyway I goes up tae see John Samuel, the heid electrician. 'Aye,' he says, 'ah've a job. Ye can start on Monday.' 'Ah,' ah says, 'ah could start the noo.' 'Ah,' he says, 'that'll no' dae, though.' 'No,' ah says, 'because,' ah says, 'finance enters intae this.' 'Oh,' he says, 'ye cannae get nae mair than thae folk in there'—this is the journeymen inside the shop. 'Oh, well,' ah says, 'that's nae use tae me. Ah'm no' daein' that. Ah'm no' comin' doon, ah'm gaun up the wey.' 'Oh, well,' he says, 'I dinnae think ye'll get any mair.' So he says, 'Go up and see Mr Mackay.' 'Very good,' ah says, 'that's no' a big job.'

Ah'd been up the stair before—but for breakin' lamps on the pit bottom. I wis fined ten shillins, for smashin' lamps, comin' through on the powny's back—phew-phew-phew-bang-bang-bang.

Onywey, when ah come oot the door that day, ma faither says: 'Ah'll tell ye something. Ah'll gie ye a tip. When ye gaun in,' he says, 'Mungo Mackay'll be sittin' at the table tap-tap-tap-tap-tappin' the table. An',' he says, 'he'll be readin' and he'll be writin' wee bits in the margins o' what he's readin', takin' notes.' 'Oh, aye.' 'Div ye ken what that's for?' ma faither says, tap-tap-tap-tap-tappin' on the table again. 'I've an idea,' ah says, 'that'll be tae make me birl ma bonnet in ma hand likely and make him think that ah'm fair nervous?' 'Well,' ma faither says, 'ah'll tell ee what. There's a big drawin' on the wall, for,' he says, 'ah wis up there a fortnight ago. And it's got a bit cut oot. It's J.B. or somebody.' 'No, no,' ah says, 'it's BJD—British Jeffrey Diamond coal-cutter. There's yin ben the hoose there, man, in ma book.' And ah brings it oot. 'There ye are—is that the thing?' 'Aye,' says ma faither, 'that's what's on the wall. If ye dinnae bother aboot him jist tappin',' he says, 'gaun forrit and look at the drawin'. Then, make him imagine ye're gaun tae take a step forrit. Then,' he says, 'he'll pull ye up.'

'Ye know what ye're up here for?' That's what ah got frae Mungo Mackay when ah wis gaun tae take a step forrit. 'No,' ah says, 'ah hivnae been told,' ah says. 'Ah wis told tae come up by Mr Samuel.' 'Uh huh. Mr Samuel's got a job for you.' 'Ah, but,' ah says, 'there's a wee bit o' snags—financial.' 'Hmmm. You want more?' 'Ah certainly do,' ah says. Ah says, 'Ah'll tell ee what ah'm wantin',' ah says, 'and you'll likely chase iz but ah cannae help it,' ah says. 'Ah want a half more than what ah've got just now.' 'Ye'll never get that!' says Mackay.

So—interview over, and ah'm nearly gaun doon the stair. He says, 'Ye'll be goin' tae leave the Lothian Coal Company?' Ah says, 'No' if ah can help it,' ah says. 'I like the Lothian Coal Company,' ah says, 'ah've been here a' ma days. Ah've never been naewhere else. But,' ah says, 'ah've got some good contacts. Ah know Mr B.P. Mackay o' Bruce Peebles, ah know Mr Henderson o' Bruce Peebles, ah know Mr Scott MacLennan o' Scottish Oils, and—ah made a mistake—ah says, 'ah know Mr Carlow Reid.' Agh! I'd taken a rid rag tae the bull when ah said that—Carlow Reid o' Fife![17]

'Ye're not goin' there! Ye're not goin' there!' Ah says, 'Ah'm no' gaun naewhere if ah can help it. Ah'm gaun tae bide here if ye'll let iz.'

So he gien iz a line, efter a wee bit wrangle, he gien iz a line and says: 'Take that tae Eckie Paxton. Now,' he says, 'ah've heard about ye before.' 'Oh?' 'Yes. You were to take a letter from a teacher to another teacher and you didn't take the letter.' 'Oh,' ah says, 'that's a while ago,' ah says, 'that wis when ah wis at the school.' 'Yes,' Mungo Mackay says, 'ah know what it was. Why didn't you take the letter?' 'Because,' ah said, 'she had doubted ma integrity and honesty. She had sealed it and it had never been sealed before. So,' ah says, 'if ah'm takin' that tae Alex Paxton and ye seal that,' ah says, 'it'll jist bide there,' ah says, 'for ah'm no' gaun tae take it.'

So he didnae seal the letter and ah went ower tae Alex Paxton wi' it. And Alex says, 'Oh, ma God, Wullie,' he says, 'oh, that's never happened before. Oh, it'll never happen again.' 'Ah cannae tell ee what's in't,' ah says, 'Ah'm tae take back a verbal answer, yes or no, or arranged or what. Ah'm jist tae tell him what you say.' 'Aye, well,' says Alex, 'gin back and tell him that'll be a'richt.'

So ah went up and telt Mungo Mackay, 'Mr Paxton says that'll be a'richt.' He says, 'Go down and get John Gilmour.' This was the heid cashier. 'Ye know him?' 'Aye,' ah says, 'ah ken him.' 'Yes,' says Mungo, 'you've wrangled wi' him before.' Ah says, 'Ah ken that. He had no richt tae keep money off o' me when he wouldnae itemise it.' So ah went doon and got John Gilmour and he came up and we had a wee confab. 'Go down wi' Mr Gilmour,' Mungo Mackay says, 'and he'll give you the instructions.' And John Gilmour says, 'When you come ower you'll hae twa lines frae Eckie Paxton.' 'Twa?' ah says. 'Aye,' he says, 'ye'll have two lines. Bring them to me or Bert Smith.' Well, ah had a crack wi' Bert and he says: 'Ye jist get yin box, mind,' he says. Ah says, 'That'll be a' ah'm wantin' if there's somethin' in't.' 'There'll be something in't,' he says, 'and ah'll tell ee something,' he says, 'what he telt me. That immediately ye get it ye go right up the stair and see him.' 'Oh, aye.'

Ah gets ma pey line. Ah had 9/6d. per shift—so there ye are. And the wage was 6/3d. Ah cannae say nothin' aboot Mr Mackay, nothin' at a'. Ah never asked for an increase, no, no, ah never asked for an increase a' ma time. Ah got it. It wis through Mr Samuel, of course. It wis him that wis aye pittin' iz up and up and up. Oh, ah had a bigger pey than onybody. Ah had a bigger pey than the manager!

So ah saw the Green Table. But that wis the only bit that interested me about the Green Table, him wi' the pincil, tappin'. And that's what it was for, so that ye'd keep birlin' yer bonnet in yer haunds and no' kennin' where ye was an' gettin' a' nerves.

Oh, there were some worthies in the pit then, though. There wis old Jock Ferrier. Old Jock Ferrier left the Lady Victoria and he went tae Fife. And he wis in digs and the woman says, 'How d'ye like yer egg, Mr Ferrier, in the morning?' 'Baith thegither, hen,' he says, 'baith thegither.' He wis only gettin' yin, ye ken.

And another man, they ca'ed him Macintosh Moffat, he stayed in Newtongrange. Well, Mackintosh Moffat, they ca'ed him Toshie Boy. There were also Pasteboard—he was Eck Moffat. There was Mosh Moffat, and they called him Auld Moshie Moffat. And there were Buck Moffat and Weesh Moffat. Onyway, somebody says tae Toshie: 'Toshie, ye dinnae work very much.' 'No, ah work plenty,' he says. The man says, 'How d'ye feed?' 'Oh,' he says, 'ah hae a bit biled egg on in the mornin'.' 'Oh, aye? A biled egg? Ah, but,' the man says, 'ye've twa or three bairns, haven't ye?' 'Ah've got three,' says Toshie. 'And what div they get?' 'A dip o' the bree,' he says. That wis the water that the biled egg was in—a dip o' the bree. Oh, ma God, he was an awfy man thon, Toshie Boy.

His son, they ca'ed him the Diamond Bore. He had a bowler hat, wi' nae rim on it, and 'Diamond Bore' across it and a hole in't for his lamp. Oh, there were some cures.

Oh, dear, Pasteboard was much the same. And there wis a man ca'ed Bobby Loudon in Newtongrange in thae days and he had twa kettles, one at each side o' the hob, big kettles for bilin' the water. And he ca'ed yin kettle Peter Dixon, and the other yin was Wullie Carson. That was the under-manager and manager respectively o' the Lady Victoria pit. 'Ah, Peter,' he says, 'that's no richt, Wullie. That's no' what he said tae me.' And that's hoo Bobby Loudon cairried on, speakin' tae hissel' and speakin' tae the twa kettles.

The contractin' system in the pit was in a sense a bad thing, because one man had power ower a' the lot. Ah'm gaun tae mention names tae ye. There's a garage at Newtonloan, the bottom o' Newtonloan. They call it William Allan's Garage. And that garage wis excavated by his ain men and he peyed them, his own men, on the Saturdays. And at the same time he could get his ain men tae dig his gairden.

Ah kent a man that worked in the Dalhousie section o' the Lady Victoria pit. He wis in the pool, it wis penny aboot and they had guid wages while they were workin' wi' Wull Shaws. And this man left tae gaun tae Wullie Allan's section. And sometimes when he came hame he couldnae pit a peen on his heid on his breeks, and that was pure sweat because there were nae water in the splint, 'cause ah wis often in the splint. And this bloke had tae take his claes off ootside afore he went in the hoose. He daurnae gaun in wi his pit claes on.

But Wullie Allan could terrorise men. He was a guid contractor—if, if, if. Ah mind o' bein' in yin day at a switch of his—there was somethin' wrong wi' the switch. Now they must have had a wee bit o' bother in the mornin' wi' the lack o' tubs or empties and they had tae take their piece quick. They must ha' had their piece maybe about a quarter past eight. And when ah went in it wid be aboot, oh, half-past ten or somethin'. Ah wis sent in because there wis somethin' wrong wi' the conveyor. Wullie Allan says tae me, 'Somethin' wrong—will ye gaun in and see it?' Ah says, 'Ah'll gaun in the noo.' That's what he wis waitin' on, of course, because ah couldnae be bothered wi' Wull Allan sometimes. Yayayayaya—'Flaming bleck poultices o' swine!' He never swore. Oh, he didnae sweir! 'Flemin' blecks, poultices and swine! A German, a Pole!' Standin' howkin' up at his lamp, tae, wi' his bare fingers! Onywey, ah gauns in, and ah'm at the switch. 'Be long, son?' 'No,' ah says, 'jist a fuse blown.' 'Have ye wire?' 'Aye, wire.' Ah put it in. Noo there were a man jist abune me and they ca'ed him Wull—ah cannae mind his other name. He stayed in First Place. But this man thocht he wid step ower the pans and take his bit piece that he had left. And Allan says: 'Hey! There no' twa piece times here, there's only yin piece time!' 'Oh,' says Wull, 'I think I can force ye to get ma piece.' 'Force yersel' up the pit the day at twa o'clock,' says Allan, 'and ah'll force a line intae yer hand!' And that bloke had tae pit his piece doon. That wis Wullie Allan. By God, man, he wis quick—lightnin', his left hand gaun, and leathering his powny, oh!

But he wi a guid contractor. I'll say that much. He wis guid tae me. He wis guid tae ma faither, tae. But he wis an awfu' man. 'Flaming blecks, poultices and swine!' Ye never heard the like o' it in yer life! Never swore, because he was a founder member o' the Tin Kirk, the Church o' Christ in Newtongrange, him and his brother David.[18] Davy was the worst. Davy wid staund if there were somethin' went wrong, smackin' his lips: 'Oh, dearie me. It's an awfy job. I'll need tae see the maister aboot this. What'll ah say?' But Wullie wid say: 'Ah'll awa' up and get some coal noo.' And he went away up the wa' and teared doon a' the loose bits. Oh, he was an awfy man, Wullie Allan. God, he wis a guid contractor. But he was the wealthiest young man in Newtongrange. A' his money wis invested. He wis an awfy man.

Then Mungo Mackay's spies. They were in the Dean Tavern maistly. They were Committee members in the Dean, ye see, and they could cairry the stories. That's where it came frae.

And it wis the Masons. Well, ah'm no Mason, of course. I never would be. There were twa men in the Dean Tavern then that ah kent wis Masons. And ma faither used tae tell iz aboot them, tae. They used tae watch a'body and he says he was sure that they cairried the stories. That wis auld John Jack and Wull Garden. Oh, there were some cures right enough. Ee could almost tell them. Ye could tell whae it wis, if ye got a story richt ye could almost tell whae it wis if ye could jist visualise or remember whae wis standin' aside ye.

Ye had tae be very careful what ye said, especially when ye wis in Easthooses. When ah went tae Easthooses first ee daurnae speak aboot onybody, because ee wid be speakin' tae a relation o' somebody else that wid jist go roond that one and it landed on tap o' you constant. They were a' connected through drink and a'thing yonder at Easthooses. Oh, it wis an awfy place.

JAMES REID

I was born in the village of Newtongrange in September 1908. I've lived there all my life.

I was at Newbattle public school till I was fourteen. Ah left on the Friday and ah started on the Monday as a despatch clerk wi' the Lothian Coal Company at the Lady Victoria pit, up in what they ca'ed the doocot. It was an office on stilts. The railway and the waggons went down through below it and we weighed them and despatched them. That was all for the princely sum of ten shillings a week, Monday to Saturday. It was in February 1923 I first had the honour of being employed by the Lothian Coal Company.

The hours of work in the weighbox were from six o'clock in the morning to nine, then ten o'clock till one, and from two o'clock till the last rake of coal came out from the pit. And you had to tare it, weigh it and put the tickets on before you got home. There were no five-day week then. It was a six-day week. We were supposed to go to the night school but all my absences from the night school was caused by the fact that I was still in the weighbridge weighing coal.

As I say, I started at ten shillings a week—fifty pence. It was a five-year apprenticeship: second year 12/6d., third year 15/-, fourth year 17/6d., and finally fifth year £1 per week.

Well, I wis only a year in the weighbox then it was straight across to the payroom, the wages office. I worked for twenty-three years in the wages office of the Lothian Coal Company, up to nationalisation in 1947.

Now I was one of a family of six. My father was a miner and so were three of my four brothers. The other brother was a blacksmith in the central workshops o' the Lothian Coal Company. My sister never had a job at all: she had to help my mother to look after the men of the family. I was the youngest, and my father thought, 'Well, he's no' goin' down the pit.' So through my marks at the school he got me a job in the office.

There were ten o' us worked in the payroom. Ye had a book, a huge book. There were fifty names in each book. And you wrote these names and the offtakes—the rent, the coal, the gas, national insurance, pipe band, brass band, Royal Infirmary. And then you wrote out an individual, except when it was a contractor. Ye got your book weighed up and ye went across and got the time book and marked the shifts in, and calculated it. Then I passed my book over to you and you checked my calculations, and vice versa.

At each page you analysed the money, in other words you went down so many. Fivers were out then. There were no such thing as anybody earnin' a fiver. You went down and counted the pound notes and wrote it. Then you went down and counted the ten shilling notes, then you counted the silver. Then when it came to elevenpence, well, that wis a sixpence, a thruppenny bit and two coppers.

Once it was all analysed and squared it went to the chief clerk, Johnny Gilmour. He phoned across to the bank, and away they went, him and the policeman in his buggy. Well, they used to get into the office at approximately nine o'clock. So I presume they would leave about six in the morning to get across to Lasswade, where the bank was, count and check the money, and bring it across. Never once, in my recollection, were they ever waylaid. It was an ideal spot for it, too, comin' round by Dalhousie. It was a horse and buggy they went in.

Well, they landed in at the office and you knew that that

was the amount o' money. Johnny Gilmour just bumped the notes, bumped the silver. You went for a £100 bag o' silver. Say there were two helpin' me, ah said: 'Right, you take that, you take the notes, I'll bring the tanners.' Ye re-checked it, laid it all out on the table and then he said, 'Right!' and you shouted: 'Number one: £1.19.11d.' He had the box ready, put the money in, and put the lid on it. He lifted your Number two—and on it went. There were no smokes then, there were no quarter of an hour piece breaks. You had to go at it hell for leather tae get rid o' that money by eleven o'clock. Occasionally, well, pound notes can stick together. So could ten bob notes, the old ten bob notes. And you would finish up a pound short. Johnny Gilmour's face used to blare up. My God, what a state tae get intae for a pound note! 'Get these checked again!' So – back to Number one. Ye switched round: I would take the book and you would open up. When ye got it ye had a sigh o' relief. Everything was hunky dory.

When I was in the pay room in the later 1920s and 1930s I was making up wages for about 3,500 men, possibly an amount of £10,000. I was looking after their coal—deductin' for their coal—handlin' cash. I was in charge o' a section eventually and ah wis bein' paid the huge amount of £2.2.6d. a week. So it was approaching slave labour.

There were no promotion. The only promotion was when somebody died and you moved up a wee bit. Well, about the time of the 1926 strike, I had about £2 a week and I thought, 'Well, ah'm responsible for 400 men's wages, offtakes, rent and the rest of it. Ah'm sure ah'm worth more than that.' And ah went in and ah asked for a rise. This was durin' the strike—the office staff were not on strike—and the Secretary, Mr J.C. Murray, told me: 'It's more like we should maybe have to pay you off. However, I'll consider it.' And, despite the huge profit the Lothian Coal Company was makin' then, about a month later they gave me the huge extra amount of half-a-crown. So instead o' ma wage bein' £2 per week it was £2.2.6d.[19]

And I may say I married at the age of thirty-three and I went in and asked for a rise then, too. And after about eighteen years' service by then I actually reached the stage I was earning £3 per week.

When ah first started work in 1923 at the weighbox I saw nothing of Mungo Mackay. When ah moved across to the office in the Wages Department after about a year or so, the only time we saw Mungo Mackay was coming in and out—but he never come into the wages room. But he always checked our books. He checked the time to see that you was doing it properly, and all the rest of it. And of course his reputation had gone before him.

Now perhaps ah should say the best to begin wi' and keep the wee bits that's not the best till the end. He was undoubtedly, in ma opinion, one o' the finest minin' engineers in Britain, not only in Scotland—one o' the best that Scotland ever had. Now he was lucky in this far, although he was a brilliant minin' engineer he also got a pit that was absolutely full o' good coal. The Lady Victoria was undoubtedly the finest pit in the Lothians. It was sunk in a good seam, beautiful coal, splint coal, jewel, whole seam coal. Mungo Mackay made sure o' one thing: he worked the best of the coal and the easiest got.

Ah remember that the Lothian Coal Company was the first in Scotland to try out an American joy-loader underground. Well, that was a forerunner of what they've got now, and we in Scotland were runnin' it first. Now that wis Mungo Mackay's minin'. He knew that had to come instead of Coal Jock shovellin' and thingmyin'—there wid eventually be machines. And that's tae his credit.

As General Manager of the three pits—Lady Victoria,

Easthouses and Lingerwood, all within a proximity of two miles—he could plan faces down the pit, he could get the coal out. He lectured at Heriot Watt College in Edinburgh. Any visitors from America—especially when they brought in the first of the mechanisation—he was there to explain it to them. He tried everything to get more coal out. Now ma father was a miner all his days and he used tae say: 'Aye, Mungo Mackay was a hard man but he knew his job.'

The result is the Lothian Coal Company prospered year after year, and Mungo Mackay eventually in Newtongrange got us away from the outside closet and gave us an inside lavatory. Instead o' us goin' out to the well for water, they gave us water in the house. They were good houses compared wi' other mining villages because any other village you visited round about here was just two single rows, with this syver running in front, and a coalhouse and outside closet. Well, he improved on that. And they reckon that by 1926 this was a model village, through the profits of the Lothian Coal Company. They had to hide them somewhere, ye see. Undoubtedly he made it a village but to give him the credit for the whole thing is wrong, because actually it was James A. Hood, the chairman of the Lothian Coal Company, who founded the Chair of Mining in Heriot Watt. He was the big fellow, the big millionaire, and he really put the plans and made them go.

Actually, if you go further back, Lingerwood, I think, and Easthouses had been owned by the Marquis of Lothian. But they found, if they went down another 300 or 400 feet, these rich seams and they sank the Lady Victoria pit, and they made a limited company, the Lothian Coal Company. The Marquis of Lothian was a shareholder. So they sank the Lady Victoria down, got the beautiful coal and made lots of profits. And the Marquis claimed royalties of sixpence a ton for every ton o' coal that came out below his ground. Now when I used to calculate the output, in a year the Lady Victoria, Lingerwood and Easthouses could produce a million ton o' coal. So that was a million sixpences—old sixpences—into the Marquis of Lothian's pocket.

So as the mining progressed, the pits o' the Lothian Coal Company at Easthouses, the Bryans, Lady Victoria, Lingerwood, and Whitehill, all prospered. And, I will admit, quite a lot of the money was ploughed back into the village to build houses and suchlike—a new public park, a bowling green, and a picture house.

But Mungo Mackay was the type that demonstrated to the full 'master and man'. He was a master's man first and foremost. There were a class which he belonged to, and there were a class that ah belonged tae. He was lord of the manor. There were no doubt about that. He was lord of the manor. Everybody walked in fear and tremblin' of Mungo Mackay. As ah say, ye didn't see much of him but ye heard the stories. He really ruled like a king in this village. He was the lord o' the manor and we were the serfs. He ruled over the village with an iron rod.

And how he did it was quite simple. He had one or two stooges. They were few and far between. And quite frankly they were held in contempt in the village. They were known, oh, they were known and they were held in contempt. It wasn't a case of a round dozen or two dozen. You could pin it down to less than that. Everybody knew that they were carrying the story. Well, one was the local policeman. He was paid half by the Lothian Coal Company and I never knew how. And then there wis—well, I can't mention names—a local head timekeeper, and that man knew everythin' that went on in the village. Aye, when ye saw him walkin' up the stairs in the office, ye jist said tae yerself: 'There's another story away up.' There were another man, who I shall leave nameless, like the head timekeeper. They were just go-betweens. Everythin' that they heard about anybody, it went up the stair to Mungo Mackay. There was another one that was employed down the pit. Mackay had another man so subservient to him that he didn't say 'Mr Mackay' when he spoke to him, he says: 'Mr Mungo Mackay, sir,' with his cap in his hand. We had another two men on the surface. One or two o' the contractors was not beyond havin' a wee chat wi' him in front o' the Green Table and tellin' him things that were o' no damned interest to them at all. He gathered his information like a military operation. You talk aboot Gestapo! He could find out about anything at all: housin', rows, what was goin' on in the village, how was the football club doin' and the bowlin' club, how was the band doin'. He jist had always that one little apple in the barrel who was prepared to speak. In the office, down the pit, on the surface, there were always one ready to run with a tale to Mungo Mackay.

As far as the village was concerned, ah don't think ah ever once in ma life saw Mungo Mackay walkin' through the village. He didn't need to—it was like the coal face: he had his informants who told him what was goin' on. He knew everything that went on in this village, because he had his snoopers planted all over the place.

You may not believe this but if you had been, say, at the Dean Tavern on the Saturday night and had a bit pint or two and went home and had a row with your wife, and the next-door neighbour heard the row and repeated it in the pit, and then one of the snoopers got hold of it and it went up the stairs to Mungo Mackay, he could send for you on the Tuesday and ask you why you were having a row with your wife and to stop it! He would fine you £1, which they sent to the Royal Infirmary. Now a pound out of a wage of £2.10.0 in those days was a terrible blow. But that was one side of Mr Mackay.

Such was Mungo Mackay's power that if, say, Tom and

Harry had met in the Dean Tavern, which was the only public house in the village at that time, and had maybe a pint or two too much and had a bit fight, a pure fist fight. Now some men who did that—there were very few—could come up the pit on Monday afternoon and there were a line on their tokens: 'You've got to go up and see Mungo Mackay.' And of course they had to go up. And he gave them a dressin' down on how they should behave and all the rest of it. And if it had been a really tough fight he told them: 'Don't go near the Dean again, because you won't be served. At least for a fortnight you'll do without a drink.' Well, that's approaching dictatorship, isn't it?

And then another trick he used to do was that occasionally miners were caught smokin' down the pit. Smoking was not allowed down the pit. But in the Lady Victoria, which was practically gas-free, the men—usually when they were at the pit bottom at the end of their shift—would say, 'Aw, ah'm gaun tae have a wee smoke.' And quite often they were caught by the oversman, and the oversman of course went straight up the stair to Mungie Mackay. So the chap who had smoked, next day a note on his token: 'You've to go up the stairs.' So up in front o' the Green Table, a right good hammerin', a lecture on the dangers o' smokin', and then Mungo Mackay would say: 'I'm deducting £1 from your wages this week, to be sent to the Royal Infirmary as a donation.' And the next week of course—it was all above board—the receipt from the Royal Infirmary was put into his pay box.

Oh, there's many a man that went up in front o' the Green Table in fear and trembling when he was summoned by Mungo Mackay. Well, as ah say, ah started at fourteen years of age with the Lothian Coal Company, and the first time ah wis called in front o' the Green Table ah wis fifteen. Ah wis a very frightened wee laddie. It was the first real 'do' ah had wi' Mungo Mackay. It was a mistake in ma calculations o' the wages books. Ah checked this other chap's books and he checked ma calculations. And for some reason or other ah ticked it off as being correct. Unfortunately, I had slipped up—a man had got ten shillings too much. How Mungo Mackay found that out I don't know. But ah was summoned, up the stairs in front o' the Green Table: 'Tell Reid to come up.'

Now he always funnily enough had to have an audience. Ye never caught him sittin' himself at the Green Table. He was always sittin' wi' the policeman, a snoop, an absolute snoop. And there would be the pit manager, the under-manager and the chief engineer. So that when you went in and stood in front of this Green Table, honestly, you felt about that size. You were never asked to sit. You just stood and you listened to what he had to say. And nobody said a word but Mr Mackay. Everybody—his oversmen, his under-managers—ah don't know how but you got the impression that they lived in fear of that man. It was an eerie experience, standin' and lookin' at six or seven men who never opened their mouths. He did all the talkin'.

So—'Tell Reid to come up.' On that first occasion Mungo Mackay was alone. He was standin' behind that famous Green Table wi' a stick in his hand. And he went completely berserk. He got out his stick and the pay book and he thumped that table. God knows, it went on for about five minutes. And what he called me and my writing and my calculations I couldn't repeat here. But I jist stood and took it all. Well, ye see, in the 1920s a job was a job. There were three million unemployed, I believe. And even although you were paid, as the saying goes, in thruppenny bits, it wis a job.[20]

On another occasion ah got the job of takin' round a collection book for this chap who was bein' married but whom Mungo Mackay detested. So ah went to everybody in the office and ah took it up this morning to his room, rapped on the door, and he was sittin' with the policeman and another man. 'Ah, well?' he says, clearing his throat. Ah said, 'Well, ah'm collectin' for so-and-so for he's gettin' married.' Ah laid the wee collection book in front o' him on the Green Table. And ah just happened to turn and look out the window. A second later ah got the book right on the side o' ma face. 'Take that away!' he says. 'Ah'm not givin' anything.'

I remember one miner who had been called up in front o' the Green Table. He had been off his work. It was the old tale: they'd taken that much off in off-takes that they had left the chap wi' about five shillins—25 pence. Mungo Mackay came down the stairs and this miner followed him and he was sobbin'. He was askin' Mackay, 'How can ah keep my wife and my children off five shillins a week?' And Mackay told him: 'Get out! Out!'

Now Mungo Mackay had his chief clerk, Johnny Gilmour, trained in the very same way. Because ah remember another man bein' off and we paid them out then in small tin boxes. We made up the money and then we stood at the window o' the office and as they came up the pit we paid them out. Ah paid this man out. Ah rattled his box: there were one penny in it. He came back—well, ah knew him—and he said, 'Aw, Jim,' he says, 'ah know ah've been off work, but my God.' So I turned to Johnny Gilmour, the chief wages clerk, and ah says: 'Look, this chap's worked five shifts,' ah says, 'ye've left him wi' a penny.' 'He's got his dues to pay to the Company. He's due the Company two tons o' coal, he's due £2.10.0d. for gas, and he's due four weeks' rent.' 'But,' ah says, 'ye could've let him off surely wi' a wee bit? Ye could have left him wi' a £1 note?' 'No!'

Well, I don't know how I didn't get the sack that day, because I completely blew my top. But the man had to go away wi' his penny.

Mungo Mackay and the Green Table

The Green Table was about fifteen feet by four, almost bigger, I would say, than a billiard table. It occupied at least a quarter of Mungo Mackay's room. The size of the table was purely and simply to spread out the maps of the underground seams, to check over with the surveyors and suchlike. Mungo Mackay had a fairly large room, and actually all that was in it was some minin' books and this big table, green covered. He sat behind it and when you were summoned you stood in front o' it.

As ah've said, Mungo Mackay ruled Newtongrange with a rod of iron. To do so, he created divisions between his staff in the office, and he also created divisions among the miners by the contracting system.

Now I was just nothing, I was just absolutely nothing to Mungo Mackay because I was a wages clerk. Ah may be biased but he always gave me the impression that I was beneath him. He must have given the miners the verra same impression, must have. Ah used tae pal about with an apprentice surveyor. He worked up the stair and I worked down in the wages room. Ma pal, because he was an apprentice surveyor, he was all the good boys of the day. Eventually he was comin' into minin', ye see, whereas ah wis gaun tae spend the rest o' ma days workin' at figures.

Then there was an incident that happened in the pay room—one o' the clerks went off the rails and was fined in the courts. I suddenly realised that, like the other ten clerks in the wages room, I didn't even know the wage of my neighbour sittin' at the next desk. I didn't know the wage of the Chief Wages Clerk. But ah didn't know other things either. And ah didn't find these things out until ah started a rent book when nationalisation came in 1947. Ah found then that some people in the office had been payin' no rent and no gas. Others were payin' rent but had free gas. Others were payin' rent but no rates. The manager, for instance, would have free rent, free gas, free coal, free sticks. And as you came down the list you would have free rent, free sticks until you came down to—well, when ah got married ah had nothing free at all. Ah had tae pay ma rent, ma rates, ma gas. Now that was probably because ah refused to be one of the snoops.

Mungo Mackay lived in Lingerwood House, right opposite the entrance to the Lady Victoria colliery. And immediately below him there were six or eight houses called The Saughs. The managers and under-managers and the Chief Engineer stayed in The Saughs. Now their gardens were all done by a labourer, their hedges were trimmed by a labourer. That was all what ye call perquisites. If ye was on the staff ye could get a bag o' sticks, a beautiful big bag o' chopped sticks to keep ye goin'—if ye had the right side o' Mungo Mackay's face. Ah never got sticks. And another difference he made with the staff was when you were married and ye paid rent and rates. Now at that time it was seven shillings rent and 1/9d. rates, year after year. There were no increases like what there is nowadays. Well, ye suddenly found out when ye started talkin' seriously about tryin' all to be equal, that one person was payin' seven shillins, but not the rates. Another person was payin' the full thing. Another favoured person was rent-free. Now seven shillins and 1/9d. for rates in these days was really something. Then it came to the coal. Some had free coal, others paid 15/9d., plus the carriage. In other words, he set the staff one against another just the same as he did with the miners by the contractin' system. He took the staff and he tore them apart, he divided them. All these instructions, the wages clerk couldn't have done it, the Chief Clerk couldn't have done it—it had to come from above. And when it came from above, that was it. We were, well, not snappin' each other but almost.

Mungo Mackay encouraged the contracting system. That was playing miner against miner. All that he did was send for a man, call him Mr Brown. And he said, 'There's a face opening down the splint. I want you to take it. Get men and get into it and take it.' Maybe there would be thirty men, because they were huge faces, virgin coal—the finest of coal—thirty or forty men. So Brown the contractor got them together and said, 'I'll pay you 9/6d. a day.' In these days they gave each miner what they called a stent. That was, say, fifteen or so feet in length, with coal maybe three or four feet high, and you had to work it with a pick. You had to pick it and put it on the conveyor and get cleaned up. If you couldn't clean off by the time you were due to be finished you had to stay there and clean it off, with no overtime payment at all.

Well, it finished up that thirty men were being paid 9/6d. a shift and the average at the end of the day was maybe 10/6d. So the contractor was getting a shilling a shift thirty times a day, six times a week. So it was quite all right to be a contractor. Mungo Mackay played the contractor against the miner, the miner against the contractor. With the result that he got the coal out, day after day. But it was only a few contractors that benefited.

It was only latterly when nationalisation came in 1947 that I sat down one day and worked out a certain contractor's wages for the week. At that time they were payin' him 10/5d. a shift, which meant, say, for six shifts about £3. Ah worked out that the thirty men employed by the contractor were earning £3.50. That left the contractor with about £35. Now £35 in the 1920s and 1930s was a fortune. And Mungo Mackay fostered that system, he just sat behind that Green Table, and if anything went wrong, he'd say: 'What's wrong? Are ye failin' on the nightshift? Get that coal cut! And there's the tonnage I'm goin' tae give ye.'

I remember another time when this face—it was called the splint coal and was about five to five-and-a-half feet high,

good coal, and no geological difficulties—was being worked.
I happened to be on that pay book, there were about 400 men
I looked after. When I worked out the calculations, instead of
normally making 12/9d. a shift, the average per shift for the
men was 15/9d. Of course, Mungo Mackay every week
checked the books, with his timekeeper and his managers
sittin' all around him, he checked every pay book. And my
pay book came down with a note: 'This average is too high.
Deduct 200 tons from that man.' So I deducted the 200 tons,
and that brought the average down near to 12/9d.—and that
contractor never opened his mouth. If that had happened
after nationalisation in 1947 there would have been a strike
the next mornin' by everybody in the pit. But that's how
powerful Mungo Mackay was. Of course in 1947, after the
nationalised Coal Board really got down to it, the contractin'
system was wiped out completely.

I'll tell ye a good laugh about the pay. About 1914 there
were some Lithuanian Poles landed in Newtongrange. Ah
don't know how they came here but they came here tae work.
It wid be through the War. The story was that they came with
a label tied on them: 'Lady Victoria pit.' And of course they
were good workers, strong, oh, strong men. Their descen-
dants are still here, more Nitten than ah am. But they had to
be given names in English, 'cause ye couldn't spell Pader-
ewsky or somethin' like that. So the Lothian Coal Company
said to them: 'You're Joe Smith and you're Joe Campbell',
and so on. Unfortunately, there were two named John Smith.
One was on the oncost, which was 6/5d. a shift then. The
other one had a wee contract, maybe back brushin' or
brushin' a side road, with seven or eight men employed.
So he was a contractor. And this day John Smith the oncost
man came up for his wage to the roundel, the window in the
office where we paid out. And how it happened I don't know,
but he was given the contractor's bag. The poor contractor

John Smith, of course, was still down the pit. He didn't come up till later. And when he came up he got the line for 6/5d. a shift. So there wis hell tae pay! The police were sent for. Johnny Gilmour, the Chief Clerk, pranced around and cried, 'Oh, ye better get down to Johnny Smith, the oncost man's house!' And when they got down there they found him in his house absolutely miraculous! I don't know how they got the money back. But after that there was only one John Smith. The other one was John Smith Graham.

What ah can recollect about the Lithuanians is what ma father told me. They were practically all Catholic. They couldn't speak a word of English. Some of them must have brought their women with them, because ah can still remember up to ten years ago a Mrs Palovsky. And you could tell right away she was a Pole, even after sixty years, ye could tell. And the men, well, they jist learned the language. But it finished up of course that their offsprings went to the school with me and they became more Scots than I was, although they always retained their mother tongue. They could always speak Polish to their father and mother, and they could speak broad Nitten tae me. Their habits jist became the same habits as the miners'. They become one of the fraternity. But they were always referred to as incomers, because a minin' community is a very close community. Even after thirty years locals would say, 'Oh, that's Joe Smith?' 'No, no, that's Joe Palewsky. Remember, he's an incomer. He came here thirty year ago.'

They were good workers. Ma father at one time had a small contract and he had about seven or eight Poles workin' on it. Unfortunately, it didnae last long, because ma father never made any money out of this contract. The Poles used to walk down our back garden on the Saturday afternoon and said, 'Oh, David,'—that was ma father—'ma pay.' And they got a dram put down in front of them and a bottle o' beer.

The result was, before ma father finished payin' out he was half jeek. And so wis the Poles. So he gave the contract up! But ah can recollect two o' the offsprings o' the Poles that became dux o' Newbattle School.

Some people say that nobody ever came into the village in those days because of Mungo Mackay's reputation as a hard man. Now that may be so, but I very much doubt it. I've got an active enough mind and ah can remember Newtongrange actually at the beginnin' of the First World War. Everybody knew everybody in Newtongrange, because their fathers had been there before them. There was no question of, say, five or six men sayin', 'Aw, ah've had enough o' Mungo Mackay. I'm goin' up to work with the Arniston Coal Company', which was two mile further up the road. We were a community, a tightly knit community. Newtongrange remained that right up to the 1940s, the Second World War.

So it may be that instilled in these old men was the old feudalist system. Ah've read about minin' and it's a known fact that a hundred years ago they did everything except put a tattoo on you.[21] You were there, you were in their house, you were signed to whatever coal company it was, body and soul. You couldn't move. So it was maybe a backlash from that that the village of Newtongrange remained predominantly of Newtongrange people. And, as ah say, there were rivalries between the village and Gorebridge, where the Arniston Coal Company was run by Viscount Dundas. There were rivalry at football, there were rivalry at everything. After the First World War we, the people who had been born and bred in Newtongrange, referred to the people employed by the Arniston Coal Company who lived in Gorebridge and Arniston, as Germans. They in turn—with no love lost— referred to us as Chinese. I can remember watching Junior football after the end of the First World War. It was quite common then for Arniston Rangers tae meet Newtongrange

Star in the League and very often in the Scottish Cup. There would be at least 3,000 spectators there, for a Junior match. I think it was thruppence ye paid tae get in, old money. And by Jove! I've seen some kickin' matches in ma time. I never took part in them, because I was too easily knocked off the ball myself. But I always loved football. I followed Newtongrange Star all over the place. And it used tae be the highlight o' the season when they met Arniston Rangers.

Folk'll say, 'Och, they were good auld times.' They were good times in a sense—that you were a community. Everybody knew everybody, everybody cared for everybody. If a woman was havin' a child it was nothin' for my mother to send down six or seven jeely pieces for her youngsters. Ah can remember a laddie whose father worked on the oncost, which was lower wages. He used tae come down every mornin' to ma house and shout for me to go to school. Well, one mornin' it had been snowin', and in those days we went with our short trousers and bare knees and big tackety boots to the school. And he was standing at our door and there were holes in his trousers and he was blue with the cold. Now I'm not trying to boast up my mother, but she just looked out, and bein' a seamstress she gave that laddie a pair o' trousers and two thick jeely pieces when she asked him and he says, 'Ah've not had a thing tae eat this mornin'.'

Now that's another thing about those days o' Mungo Mackay. There were some fine women in the minin' community who never even saw down the pit but they knew all the agonies of it and the bitterness—especially during times o' strikes. Without any boastin' I had a wonderful mother. Ah can't recall her ever havin' a holiday outside Newtongrange until all the family were up workin' and ah wis well over twenty. The simple reason was she was devoted to her family. They all came in dirty to the house. Now the back kitchen was just a cement floor, a boiler, and a hand basin. There was nothing else. And that boiler had to be filled every day with hot water, waitin' for ma father and the three brothers tae come wi' their dirty pit clothes that they cast off. And my mother washed their backs. When I was old enough I washed my father's back—and I was proud to do so. There were no showers. Ye couldn't get the coal dust off your back unless it was washed off by another member of the family.

There were eight of us in my family, countin' ma father and mother. Ye know what cooking that meant. It was the old-fashioned great big fire, two ovens on either side. All the meat was made there. You had tae go outside for the water. And when my sister left school the work was so plentiful in the house that my mother couldn't let her go out and look for a job. My sister is 75 now and she's never had a paid job in her life. She just looked after the family along with my mother until such times as she got married, then the old cycle began again. So ah take off ma hat tae the women of the minin' community. I can assure you o' that.

The worst poverty ah saw in Newtongrange in these years was at the time o' the miners' strikes in 1921 and 1926. In the 1921 strike ah used to run home from the school and the miners used to meet in Newtongrange Star's park, hundreds o' them. And a leader would stand up and say: 'Just hold out another week and we'll be there.' And ah remember one miner standin' up wi' tears in his eyes, and sayin': 'Who is goin' to get ma six children their next meal?' Now that's poverty. And that man had the guts to stand up and say it. But there were hundreds like him.

In 1921 I was thirteen and me bein' a sort o' senior pupil at the school ah had tae stay behind and ladle out the mince to the youngsters. It was a huge basin o' mince, and we fed the schoolchildren. One day—ah stayed right in the main street—and there were an awful commotion. This was the miners walkin' up through the village wi' their staves o' wood, real belligerent—not Newtongrange miners, they had come from all over. They walked right through the village and they got up to the Lothian Coal Company office and it looked pretty bad. I followed them up to see what was goin' on. They walked up and they said: 'Draw the fires!' If they had drawn the fires at the Lady Victoria the pit would have been flooded. But it was not Mr Mungo Mackay who walked through that threatening mob. It was the pit manager who had to do it and, believe me, he was a very white-faced manager.[22]

Of course, the next day the troops came in.[23] Then the Lothian Coal Company got a number o' blacklegs. They kept them within the gates and fed them like fighting cocks—steaks and everything, anything that they wanted. The story goes that the local policeman, a huge man, had the dessert—prunes—one day and they counted forty-five prune stones on the side of his plate. So that gives you an idea of how they were fed.

The miners got out the local band. They stopped and played a nice wee tune for Mr X, who stayed in Fourth Street and was up on the pit blackleggin'. They broke a window or two and put a big white slab on his door—BLACKLEG. I followed them round the village. Marking the doors was common, well, I heard of it done at other pits. That's why the blacklegs couldn't stay in the village—they would ha' got a hammerin'. So they stayed within the locked pit gates and they put in beds and everything for them. Well, I think it wis sixteen weeks the 1921 strike lasted.[24] And the entire village finished up due the Store, due the candlemaker and everything. It wis a tragedy for the working people in Newtongrange. And the blacklegs were sent to Coventry for quite a wee while—I'd say months, and then it wore off.

Then in the 1926 strike Mungo Mackay played no role at all, he played no role at all. He kept very much to his family in the big house. The 1926 strike did not do the Lothian Coal Company any harm at all. Ah happened to be working then in the offices with a man who bought Polish coal. They brought Polish coal to Leith—ye never saw it—and they sold it from there. They were buyin' in waggon loads o' coal at Leith and sellin' it and makin' a huge profit. They made a bigger profit in 1921 and 1926 than they did the year previous or the year after.[25] So the General Strike didn't perturb Mungo Mackay and the Lothian Coal Company secretary J.C. Murray in the least. The General Strike fizzled out after a week or not much more, and the miners kept goin' on but at the end of the day they gained nothing, nothing whatever. At Newtongrange the miners went lookin' for coal for their fires on the sides o' the river Esk. Ma own father did that and was put off by the landlord for takin' coal there. But there were poverty: ma sister and I had some War certificates from the First World War, and ma mother's sole possession was £200 in the Co-operative. The old Co-operative was the thing wi' the miners. Well, at the end o' the 1926 strike, ma sister's thirty or forty War certificates were gone, ma War certificates were gone, and ma mother's £200 in the Store was gone. We owed no man but we hadn't a penny in the world. The 1926 strike cleaned out an awful lot of miners from the pit. They never went back because of the length of it—seven months.

Now talking about unions: the men were represented by John Rutherford. As a youngster John had his leg taken off at the socket in an accident at the pit. He gradually took over the miners' trade union at Newtongrange. They didn't carry much weight in these days. And I've seen John Rutherford—I knew him well because he lived in the village—I've seen him standing wi' his peg leg, or walkin' up and down upstairs in the colliery offices, because he'd been sent for by Mungo Mackay or he wanted to discuss a certain thing that had happened at the pit. He was not offered a seat outside the office, I presume he would be offered a seat inside. But ah've seen him walkin' up and down that corridor for at least an hour before it came up Mr Mackay's back to see him. Many's the long wait that John Rutherford had. I don't think he ever got very far with Mungo Mackay.

I didn't dare join a trade union myself. I remember once, well, when I got to the age of about thirty—it was in Mungo Mackay's last days—and wondered what life was all about. I worked in the pay room with eight or nine wages clerks and ah says: 'Look, why, why are we not in the union?' You can believe it or not, I didn't know whether they were gettin' the same wage as me or more than me or less than me. And one time it came out when one of the clerks, as ah say, went off the straight and narrow and tried to do the Lothian Coal Company for so many pounds. In the court case his wage was mentioned. At that time I had the huge wage of £2.2.6d. a week, but this chap who was tried in court had started three year after me and he had £2.12.6d. When I found that out I said: 'What about a union?' And ah was told by the Chief Wages Clerk: 'You try—or any o' you try—to form a union and you'll be replaced. You'll be replaced.' So that we were actually cowed.

Mungo Mackay ruled by fear. I remember, for instance, there were only one door into the head office. Our hours were from nine o'clock to five. There were no overtime. At five o'clock you were cleaned up and you were out the door. Well, this day, the clock was in the hall and I was making my way out and it was one minute to five. The door slammed in my face. It was one of these swing doors. I tried to push it. It was pushed the other way—and there was Mungo Mackay. He looked at the clock. He cleared his throat as usual: 'You're a minute too early. Get back to the room.' And I had to meekly walk back into the payroom for one minute till I could get home.

Mungo Mackay always had a bad habit o' clearin' his throat—AGGHHHRRR—before saying anything at all. It was an unfortunate way of speaking to people. Bad manners it was to me, in more ways than one. It wis jist as if he had a cold and there wis flem. There wis always a wee bit flem, because it wasn't a NNNRRHHH. It was always AAGGGHHHRRR. I'm not saying there was something wrong with his throat. I don't think it ever came to anything. But he cleared his throat in high company or low company, always AAGGGHHHRRR. He forgot all about his cough when he lost his rag, of course.

He spoke very brusque. Ah can't tell ye any funny stories about him because ah think he was absolutely devoid o' humour. Ah can't remember ever seein' him smile. He was a big handsome man. He was fully six foot tall, moustache, no beard, and he walked very erect. And he always had a stick either when he went down the pit or when he was walkin' across the road to the pit or over the pithead to the blacksmiths' shop, and so on.

Ah verra, verra seldom seen him in the village. He lived a life o' his own with his wife and family. Where he went for holidays ah don't know. In fact, I never once saw Mr Mackay walk through the village, except perhaps at the opening of the public park in 1926. That was the one and only time that ah saw Mr Mackay away from the pit. I think he jist wanted tae be entirely divorced from the men, as regards their social life. In these days ye had tae make your own social life. Ye went to the cricketers' dance, the Young Men's Guild dance, the Liberal dance, or somethin' like that. Ye would get the Lothian Coal Company secretary to come, and maybe the chief accountant, the chief surveyor. But Mungo Mackay would never come—well, he did come once to the Young Men's Guild annual dance: that was the one and only time ah saw Mungo Mackay at something in the village. He never attended a funeral. I've never seen him at a funeral. I've never seen him at a weddin'. As far as religion went ah think that he went to Cockpen Church, which is out the village, ye see, maybe two to two-and-a-half mile from his house at Lady Victoria.[26] But he always had the car at his disposal, of course, and a chauffeur. Any functions, such as the Gala Day, you never saw him there. That might give the impression that he was a bit o' a loner. He was a strange kind o' man. They say he was instrumental in getting Newtongrange Park opened in 1926. Ah wis at the opening o' it by Lord Chelmsford. But Mungo Mackay wasna there.[27]

The only thing was when he came through here from Ayrshire in the 1890s they started a Masonic Lodge. And he was the first Right Worshipful Master. At that time of course the village was growing at a terrible rate. So was the Lady Victoria pit. They were always openin' other seams and they required miners. They must have thought, 'Well, we'll have our own Lodge.' His first and second degree in the Masons had been taken at Cumnock before he came through here as a young man, and he took his third degree at Bonnyrigg. And when they opened a new Lodge here he was the first Master. The second Master, funnily enough, was my uncle, who was the manager o' the Lady Victoria, William Carson. In these days it was inclined to be that the manager was then followed by the Chief Engineer and the under-manager. The Lodge was founded, I think, in 1910 and it was well into the 1920s before you got a workin' man as Worshipful Master. One of the earliest, funnily enough, was my own brother. He was the youngest Master ever in that Lodge. He was crazy about them. But once Mungo Mackay did his term I don't think he came very much about the Lodge. Of course, you normally find that. When you're a Master o' a Lodge you usually do two years and at the end o' the second year you're only too glad to get rid of it and pass it on to somebody else. When ah went through the Masons Mungo Mackay was nowhere near the place at all. But you can't blame him for that for all the past Masters that ye saw up on the board were out, too.

Finally, of course, Mungo Mackay mellowed slightly with old age. And by this time—it was 1938, just before he died—they were forming a pipe band in the village. Again ah wis sent for up to the Green Table and he said: 'AAGGGHHHRRR, Reid, they're wantin' tae start a pipe band. You will be treasurer and secretary. You'll arrange to take the money from the miners to pay up the pipes.' So ah had no option. The months went by, they practised, the pennies grew into pounds, and they got their pipes paid. Then it came to choosin' the tartan. Again he sent for me and in front of him was a big book of tartans. He went through it— MacDuff, MacGregor, MacKenzie, Maclean. 'AAGGGHHHRRR, I think we'll have the Mackay tartan.' It wis jist a mass of yellow. It was not an attractive tartan. However, ah had no say. And ah sent away by letter for sixteen kilts in the Mackay tartan. About an hour later, he sent for me again and he says, 'No, I don't like the Mackay tartan. You'd better make it the Stewart.' That's when ah broke the law. The letter ordering Mackay tartan kilts had already been put in the letterbox in the village. So ah broke even, ah may tell you, runnin' down into the village. I asked the postmaster, whom I knew very well, if he would give me that letter back out of the box. That's breakin' the law. Well, after a good bit o' coaxin' he did gaun in and gie me it back. And I was able to destroy the letter and send another: 'Please send sixteen kilts in Stewart tartan.'

Well, they got their kilts, they got their pipes, they got their drums, and they were a brave sight, ah will admit that. And they decided tae have a great openin' night down at the big hall at Lothianbridge. I had to arrange all that. By this time

Mungo Mackay was the General Manager and a Director. Ah thought, 'Well, he'll come down here tonight and listen to the band playin'.' We had a whopper o' a supper and a drink or two. The manager o' the pit at that time came. But Mungo Mackay didn't come.

Well, he was a big strong man and he lived until he was seventy anyway. I think it wis in 1938 his health deteriorated and he died the following year. Of course, the office was completely closed on the day of his funeral. He was buried in Newbattle cemetery there, and it was the old long procession, with all the miners followin'.

You'll find people in the village yet who yearn for the old days. They say, 'Oh, Mr Mackay, he was a good man.' But you'll get others of course sayin': 'The best day that happened tae Newtongrange was when he went down that brae tae the cemetery.' He was a complex character, there were no doubt about that. I didn't hate the man. I hated some of his principles—I mean, that the master was always right. But, as ah say, you'll get people in Newtongrange who yearn for the old days: 'Aw, if Mungo Mackay was back—this village is gaun tae hell now.' Maybe so, but ye can put your foot on a man's neck just a bit too hard, you know. That's what ah thought he did.

ROBERT PEARSON

The Lady Victoria it was started sinkin' in 1890 and in 1894 it started producin'. My paternal grandfather he was born in 1858 and he worked in agriculture at Dewarton, near Pathhead. And when the Lady Victoria was opened in 1894 he came over here to Newtongrange and secured a job at the Lady Victoria. So he was really the first miner in our family. He walked back and forward from Dewarton every day, ten miles a day he walked.

My father was born in 1887 at Dewarton. His two brothers and two sisters were all born there as well. My father went to Cranston school near Dewarton. After a while, when my grandfather was workin' at Lady Victoria, the Lothian Coal Company started to build more houses here in Newtongrange. See, at one time there was only what they termed Abbeyland at the foot o' the village. That was the only houses that were in there and they were originally built in connection with the paper mill at Lothianbridge. Then the first houses that the Lothian Coal Company built were in Dean Park, over at the railway side. And then they started to build the houses in Sixth Street. Frae there right up to Lingerwood Road, that was all called Monkswood. My grandfather got one of the houses there and then the whole family came to Sixth Street, No. 9 Sixth Street, just opposite where the church is and next door to Adam Haldane's family. They were brought up together, Adam Haldane and my dad. After my grandfather came to Newtongrange to live, my father and his brother

Tom got jobs down the Lady Victoria too. That was their first job. That would be about 1900.

When my grandfather started at the Lady Victoria in 1894 the sections werenae driven. They were just driving them at that time. He worked the points at the pit bottom, where the hutches came off the cages and were being diverted—one to Carrington section and one to Dalhousie, and others to the splint, that sort of thing. That was his first job. He was an oncost worker. He was never actually a face worker. He was one of the forerunners o' workin' at Lady Victoria, as they were just startin' tae drive the pit.

I knew both my grandfathers. My other grandfather, he was a brassfinisher. He belonged Edinburgh. I remember my grandfather Pearson talkin' about workin' in the Lady Victoria. But I can't say I remember him saying anything about Mungo Mackay. I was too young then to remember anything aboot that. Grandfather Pearson died in 1920, when I was nine.

When my father and his brother Tom started work in the Lady Victoria about 1900 their first jobs down the Lady was to break away sections and drive sections in—start sections for gettin' into the coal. They were in pretty well at the beginnin' o' the colliery like my grandfather Pearson. So my father became a face worker.

In fact, I can remember one day he'd been workin' at the parrot coal—a two-feet seam, lying on his stomach. And the parrot had burst out and it got him right down there in his shoulder. He came home and he had to get fourteen stitches in his arm and shoulder. It left yon blue marks that parrot leaves, right down that shoulder. That blue scar remained with him for life. I can sit here and picter that wound right down there. They'd put a bandage on it but he took the bandage off when he came home and I seen it then. Aye, that blue scar was a lifer for him. I seen it when he had his bath. In these days we jist had a tin bath that we bathed in. There were no baths or anythin' in thae days in the houses. So the miners jist had a tin bath and they used to have a big kettle on the hob, wi' a big what we called a jarry in it to keep the fur frae collectin' in the kettle. The jarry was made o' the same material—stoneware—that the jam jars were made o' at that time, so we called it a jarry.

My father was secretary of the union, the Miners' Federation, the Newtongrange Branch. He would be about the first secretary of it when the Miners' Federation was formed, I believe. Him and John Rutherford and John Hamilton, who were the three mostly inveigled in it, they used to go up to the Green Table and fight for the rights of the miners often. Well, I was pretty young at that time and I didnae pay a great deal of attention to anything that was said. But during the 1921 strike—it was a bad strike—I went wi' my barra, along wi' my father, and we went round the shops jist in Newtongrange collectin' stuff, and bones frae the butcher, for the soup kitchen. My father and my mother they were inveigled in the soup kitchen. My father was active in the union at that time.

I was born in April 1911 so I'd be ten when the 1921 strike took place, goin' wi' ma barrae round the shops. Ma barra was jist made oot o' boxes, jist two wheels and a couple o' trams for a handle. Quinto the ice cream man, an Italian, he was very good to the village at that time. He used tae give my father boxes o' yon Nestle's chocolate tae sell for the bairns, penny and tuppenny bars. When the miners were on strike it wis the shopkeepers' livin' too, ye see, that was suffering.[28]

The soup kitchen was doon at the Lothian Hall. That wis the only hall at the time in the village, though the Picture House was built in 1915. The Band Hall was built later on. I went down jist aboot once a day. We got soup, made wi' the bones usually. It kept us goin', kept us goin'. Other meals, well, your mother had to rustle up somethin', a rabbit or somethin'. There were a lot o' rabbits caught in these days. I never went out myself tae catch them but there was a man— Jeffrey they called him—he used tae go away up there on his bike and he used tae come back doon through Newtongrange—ye couldnae see him for rabbits! They were all over his handle bars and round about him. He caught them wi' traps and he used tae sell them to folk roond aboot. He was a miner, but he used to do that often at the weekends and whenever he could get spare time. And I remember the soldiers being brought out to Newtongrange in the '21 strike. They were up on the mineral railway bridge, jist at the top o' the village, across the A7 road. They were guardin' that bridge.

I remember the 1926 strike tae. You see the bing down there? Nitten-by-the-Bing, they used tae call it. Well, my uncle Tom, my father and I used tae go down there and dig down intae the bing and try and get a good bit where there wis coal. If ye got a good bit ye stayed there all day, diggin'. I used tae come up wi' ma bike, put a bag through the handlebars and maybe take a bag up to our coalhoose, and then the next bag up to uncle Tom's coalhoose, the next bag up to uncle Dave's coalhoose. The Lothian Coal Company didnae try to stop us takin' coal frae the bing.

My father wasnae victimised after the 1921 strike and he wasnae in the pits by 1926. Because at the back end o' 1925 the doctor said: 'Ye've tae get out the pit.' It was pneumoconiosis, swallowing the coal dust. He says, 'You must get out the pit.' So my father was off for a while then he got the job of assistant registrar. So he never went back to the pits after 1925. He had to give up the union, of course, but he was a man that had always needed to be into something like that. He was a member o' the School Board for a long time and he was twenty-two years on Gorebridge Co-operative Society committee. He always had to be active in village life. He was on the committee o' Newtongrange Star football club when they won five cups out o' six one year. And he was in the Masons and my uncle Dave was secretary o' the Masons. So our people have been active in the village life more or less all our life.

As far as I remember, my father got on very well with Mungo Mackay. I don't remember much aboot the early days, I just remember my father and the other members of the Miners' Committee goin' up tae the Green Table and, well, of course, they didnae come back and say very much tae me aboot it. But I can't say I have any recollections of my father being very critical of Mungo Mackay. The Miners' Federation were very, very strong in this locality at that time and, as I say, my father and Mr John Rutherford, the president, and John Hamilton, they were often up fightin' for the rights o' the miners. And very often they came away successful.

I left school—the old Newbattle school—when I was fourteen. I thoroughly enjoyed my school days. I must say I liked the teachers. My best subject was composition. The dux o' the school, him and I used tae vie to see whae could get the biggest words to put in our compositions, oor stories. And I was quite good at dictation and spelling. I would have liked to stay on at the school, but in these days, well, wages were very, very poor and it was expected that you went to work as soon as possible.

I was keen to be a motor mechanic, which was out of the ordinary. My father mentioned this to Mungo Mackay when he said he had a boy leavin' the school shortly. Mungo Mackay said, 'Oh, well, there are no jobs up here for a motor mechanic. And you know as well as I do that I like the boys to come into the mines.' So nothing more was said then. But two or three days later Mungo Mackay sent for my father. He had taken the trouble to see if he could get a job as a motor mechanic for me. That was very unusual for Mungo Mackay and showed that he had another clock, ye see. I don't know whether it was because he was impressed wi' my father or no'. It wisnae like him to do such a thing. Possibly, it might have been because my father was the union branch secretary and he was tryin' to influence him in some way, it might have been. In fact, when my father came back to him and said that because I was to get only five shillings a week as an apprentice motor mechanic at the job at Portobello Mungo Mackay had found for me he couldnae afford to put me tae that job, Mungo Mackay said to my father, 'Well,' he says, 'say nothing more to anybody about it.'

So two or three days after that again my father was sent for. There was a job as an apprentice electrician underground in Lingerwood pit if I wished to take it. So that's where I started, Lingerwood, in 1925, when I left school. I went down the pit just about the time my father had to leave the pits because of his health.

I started at Lingerwood with Mr David Kerr. Well, he was only about a year there when he went away to Australia and Andrew Garrett was the next electrician, transferred from the Lady Victoria up to Lingerwood. I served wi' him for another year. And at that time you served so long as an apprentice in Lingerwood, so long on the surface, then so long down the Lady Victoria, then back to the surface to finish your five-year apprenticeship. So that's what I did. I finished my apprenticeship and came up to the surface again and was in the workshops for a while.

As I've said, as far as I remember, my father got on very well with Mungo Mackay. And all the time that I knew him and worked there I got on very well with him, too. I remember one time they built other two rooms and a bath-room on to the big house, Lingerwood House. So one day Mr Samuel, the chief electrician, he shouted me over in the workshop. 'Come wi' me.' So we landed over in Lingerwood House. The brickies and the plasterers had been over putting this addition on. He took me up the stairs to the addition and he says, 'You think you could wire this place up?' Well, we hadn't done any o' that work, it was all colliery work we done. 'Oh, well,' ah says, 'ah'll have a go at it.' Eventually I got the job finished. It was a bit of a struggle doin' the bathroom because George Mackay, the son, had wanted the whole bathroom tiled. And they'd tiled it but they hadnae left any provision for gettin' wirin' or tubin' or any electrification in. However, I finally got over that by bringing it in from the outside, because he wanted a plug and a mirror put up at face height.

A little while after that I was sent over to Lingerwood House again to put a telephone extension bell in. Mrs Mackay was there and I said, 'Well, where would you like the extension bell put?' 'Oh, just put it at the foot of the stair there.' So I said, 'I don't think that's a good place,' I says, 'you'll no' hear it there. It would be better up the stair in the hall, outside your sleeping accommodation.' And just at that Mungo Mackay brushed past me. He'd come in, unbeknown tae me, and he went over to her and he chucked her under the chin. He says, 'Now, now, my dear,' he says, 'the electrician knows his job better than you do.' And he turned tae me and he said: 'You put it where ye think we'll hear it.' He was a different man in the house from what he was outside.

His wife was a lovely woman, a lovely woman. I was often over at Lingerwood House trying to do anything that needed done in the electric line, and she would say to one o' the maids—they had two maids—when I was finished the job: 'Give the electrician something out the fruit press.' She had a big deep fruit press, and they had a big garden and a big greenhouse where they grew grapes and apples and all this sort o' thing. And they used tae be stored in this big deep press. Mrs Mackay often used tae say, 'Give the electrician somethin' out the fruit press.' She wis a gem o' a woman.

Mungo Mackay outside the house—well, there was another day I remember. Every Sunday morning, most Sunday mornings anyway, he used tae take a walk around the yard, the colliery pithead, and check up on everything. And this Monday morning he cam in tae the workshops wi' a piece o' brass. It was the bottom o' a light bulb. Well, we used to have a barrel in the workshop that any old brass was thrown into and it wis eventually taken up to the stores and was sold tae Finlayson, the scrap merchant in Musselburgh. The money was accredited to the colliery. And Mungo Mackay came in this Monday morning, his stick wavin'. 'Look what I've found! Look what I've found!' Somebody must have had an old bulb and thrown it down in the yard, ye see. And, oh, he went off the deep end about this, being a bit o' brass that had been left. Oh, he was a stickler, aye, oh, aye.

Another time the electrician at Easthouses wis injured and I was sent over to deputise until he was able tae come back. So this day when I went down the pit George Mackay came down. He was the General Manager o' Easthooses at that time. In the haulage there's what they term the basin. It's a dip in the haulage and the hutches were secured to the haulage rope by a chain. When it came to this bit the chains had to be taken off at the top side and the empties gravitated down into the dip and then they were chained away into the sections on the other side of the dip. So it appeared that George Mackay had said, 'I want lights in the basin, 'cause it's too dangerous for the men.' I didn't know anything about this, of course, and he got on to me when he came in. 'Oh,' I says, 'I don't know anything about it.' 'Come up and see father,' he says, 'come up and see father.' However, I had occasion to go away tae a breakdown in one o' the sections and I was late in gettin' up the pit. So by the time I got up the pit and cycled home, got my dinner and washed, it was pretty late. So I didnae bother goin' up tae the Green Table. The next mornin' the under-manager, Davie Carson, came tae me. 'Here,' he said, 'you wis tae go up the stair yesterday.' I explained tae him what had happened. 'Well,' he says, 'ye've tae go up this afternoon.' So up I goes tae the Green Table and George Mackay was in wi' his father. 'Oh, yes,' he says, 'it's about those lights in the basin, father. They're not up yet,' he says, 'they've not been put up.' And he says, 'It's about a month ago since I spoke about it.' So Mungo Mackay turns to me: 'Well, Pearson, what have you to say about that?' 'Well,' I says, 'I've only been sent over there temporary, Mr Mackay. But as far as I'm aware the materials have been ordered.' Because, fortunately, I'd gone over to see my boss, Mr Samuel, and acquainted him wi' the situation. Mr Samuel says tae me, 'That stuff's been ordered and,' he says, 'you go up the stair and if you've any trouble tell Mr Mackay to phone me across.' So when I went in tae the Green Table, 'Well,' ah says, 'as far as I'm aware the material's been ordered. But until such time as I get the material I cannae do anything.' So Mungo Mackay pressed one o' the bell pushes under the Green Table. And Jimmy Liddell, the buyer, came in. He was ordered tae bring up his order book, which he did. 'Look up and see if there's any lightin' material for Easthouses ordered up.' So the order was looked up: 'Yes. Twelve lightin' fittings, 200 yards o' lightin' cable.' So Mungo Mackay turned to me: 'That's all right, Pearson,' he says, 'ah'll see that you get the material. You see that you get the job done. Ok,' he says, 'off you go.' See, whenever ye were in the right, ye didn't need to be afraid to go up to the Green Table and face him.

Another time, when I was down Lingerwood pit, I was givin' the haulage man a hand to put a hutch on that was off the road. Ah went in between them to put my weight on, you see, and he put a stone at the wheel. But unfortunately it slipped out and ah wis squeezed between the hutches. Ah got a rib broken and ma wrist broken. And at that time you were usually off on compensation, when you had to be in at nine o'clock at night then. And ye didnae get started work again until ye went up tae the Green Table and seen Mr Mackay. So I was duly ready to be signed off. I went up and finally got in to see Mr Mackay about startin' work. Of course he quizzed me about what had happened. I told him I had stopped to give the haulage man a hand because he was strugglin' tae get the hutch on and it was on an incline. So he turned to me: 'Well, Pearson. We appreciate the fact that you were tryin' to keep the work goin' and to help out. But,' he says, 'your job is an electrician and see that you stick to your job in future. Right, off you go, across to the timekeeper and tell him it's o.k. to get started again.'

I didnae have any encounters wi' Mungo Mackay when I was disciplined by him because I had been in the wrong. Every time that I had anythin' to do wi' him I had my facts at my finger ends. I was ready. I believe that the majority o' the miners did think he was tyrannical a bit, ye see. But then again, to me, he was tryin' to make the pit a real pit, the best pit that was possible.

I mean, one o' the conditions that an apprentice started at was that he must go to the night school. And if he didn't attend the night school or was off any length of time, his father was sent for to bring his boy up to the Green Table. And things wis sorted out then: 'Why was the boy not attending the night school?' And maybe the father didnae even ken that the boy was goin' out the house but no' attendin' the night school. Mungo Mackay would know if an apprentice wasn't attending the night school because the night schools would probably be alerted, if there was any prolonged absence, to notify the colliery.

You went to different night schools. I went two years to

1. Mungo Mackay in his regalia as Grand Master of Lodge St Mary's, Newbattle.

2. Mungo Mackay seated bareheaded to left of Lord Chelmsford (standing) at the opening of Newtongrange public park in 1926.

LOTHIAN MINERS FLOCK TO HEAR THEIR LEADER.

3. A.J. Cook, General Secretary of the Miners' Federation of Great Britain, addressing 5,000 miners in Dalkeith public park on 7 August 1926 during the great national lock-out of the miners from April to November that year. Courtesy of Mr Anderson, 3 Lothian Street, Bonnyrigg.

4. Electricians at Lady Victoria colliery, Newtongrange, 1920s.

5. Miners on their way home from Whitehill colliery, Rosewell, mid 1920s. Courtesy of Mr James Lannan, 4 Hopefield Place, Bonnyrigg.

6. Soup kitchen organisers and staff at Newtongrange during the three-month lock-out by employers of miners throughout Britain in 1921.

7. Reading room , Miners' Institute, Newtongrange.

8. Lady Victoria pit head, Newtongrange.

9. Lady Victoria pit bottom, Newtongrange.

10. Housing at Monkswood, Newtongrange in the early 20th century.

11. Housing like this at Newtongrange was considered to be among the best in Scotland in the earlier 20th century.

12. Blacksmith's shop at Lady Victoria colliery, 1930s. Courtesy of Mr C. Martin, 11 Galadale, Newtongrange.

13. Colliery waggon builders at Lady Victoria colliery, c. 1943. Courtesy of Mr J. Turnbull, 44 Seventh Street, Newtongrange.

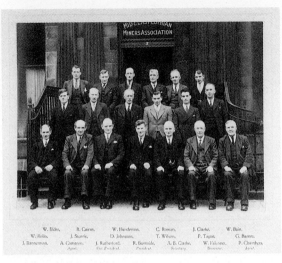

W. Elder,   R. Cairns,   W. Henderson,   C. Rowan,   J. Clarke,   W. Bain.
W. Rollo,   J. Storrie,   D. Johnston,   T. Wilson,   P. Tague,   G. Barns.
J. Bannerman,   A. Cameron,   J. Rutherford,   R. Burnside,   A. B. Clarke,   W. Falcong,   P. Chambers,
Agent.   *Vice President.*   *President.*   *Secretary.*   *Treasurer.*   *Agent.*

14. Mid & East Lothian Miners' Association Board of Delegates at their office at Hillside Crescent, Edinburgh between the wars.

15. Office staff, Lothian Coal Company, Newtongrange. James Reid, back row, extreme left. J.C. Murray, Company Secretary, front row, fourth from left.

Newbattle night school and I took mathematics there. Then I went to Leith Technical College, instead o' goin' to Heriot Watt, 'cause my cousin—he'd been to both places—advised me to go to Leith Tech, because they took more pains and more time intae ye there. I carried on at night school for about four or five years, all the time I was servin' my apprenticeship. But I never fell foul o' Mungo Mackay as an apprentice. As I say, if you were in the right and ye were doin' your job ye were o.k.

When ye did go up the stairs tae see him he was seated at the Green Table. It was a pretty long table, longer than the average table. It had been made actually in the colliery. My wife's grandfather was the head joiner with the Lothian Coal Company at that time and it would be made under his jurisdiction, I expect. It was a long table but ah wouldnae say it was actually baize it wis covered wi', it was shiny, shiny—more like an oil cloth. Well, he sat behind the Green Table and he looked pretty severe. Frank Taylor—he was the policeman, half employed wi' the local Constabulary and half employed by the colliery—he was as often up there in the office as he was anywhere. And he was often sent to people's houses if any discipline was to be enacted.

I think a lot of the people in Newtongrange thought Mungo Mackay was a bit of a tyrant. That's right enough. But they actually wouldnae be in contact with him, ye see, but maybe some disciplinary action that he had caused to be done would maybe affect them. And then of course in these days if ye had got a house in the village ye had to do your garden. Now if you didn't do your garden there was a man sent to do it and if you were fined the fine was sent to the Royal Infirmary. My father was never in trouble with Mungo Mackay over the garden. I used tae dig the garden. I used tae come home frae the school at dinner-time. Our garden wasnae very big down at Fourth Street and I could very near dig the most o' it. The ground was that soft and easy tae work. Ah could dig it over no bother as a schoolboy.

I can't say I have any recollections o' evictions at all. I mean, up tae I left the school I don't remember any evictions. Possibly there wis while I wis at school but I don't remember any evictions after ah started work.

As soon as you started work at the colliery you were expected to join the union, the Miners' Federation. I was a member as soon as I started work. I cannae remember any particular cases involving union members getting into maybe a disagreement wi' Mr Mackay or being disciplined. I was on the branch o' the Tradesmen's Association for three years and Adam Haldane was president at that time. If we had a local meetin' Adam and Bill Carson used tae go up after and discuss things wi' Mungo Mackay that had been broached at the branch meetin'. It was left to them to carry out anythin' and they brought it back to the next meetin'.

I was never fined at the Green Table. Any o' the men that were fined, I think they jist took it as a matter o' fact. They just accepted it. If it had been goin' tae the colliery or somethin' like that . . . but, ah mean, it wis goin' tae a good cause. In fact, there is a plaque up in the Infirmary aboot it in the corridor, a big plaque, that it was sent frae the Lothian Coal Company.

I cannae remember any o' my workmates bein' called up to the Green Table, no' really. Well, us bein' tradesmen, we werenae up at the Green Table so very often, especially the surface workers, ye see. It was more the underground workers.

Mungo Mackay used to come round the village himself. He used tae walk up the backs—not so much these ones around Seventh Street, because these houses werenae built until 1924. This was the first street that was built then. And it was only after the houses were all built that Mungo Mackay used tae take an occasional walk round about tae see the state o' the village, if the gardens were being dug.

As a matter of fact, I think that the tenants were chosen to a certain extent, if they were requirin' a house, where they would be put. 'Cause, when we were in Fourth Street, there were my father then there was a contractor next door, then there was a fireman the next door, then there was another contractor the next door, ye see. To me it looked as if the tenants had been picked, stayin' next door in that street, tae a certain extent. It wasnae the case that the surface workers lived in some streets by themselves and that the underground workers were put into other streets, and the tradesmen in others again. No, jist maybe a certain part o' the street and then it would be a mixed bag.

Some o' the houses were built for the deputies and firemen. They were bigger and better houses. The houses in The Square—my wife's grandfather, being head joiner o' the Lothian Coal Company, he did live in the top house in The Square. These big houses on the far side, the top side o' The Square, was where the gaffers usually lived. They lived round The Square and then the ordinary miners were in the other streets.

Newtongrange was a strong Labour village, oh, undoubtedly, undoubtedly. Mungo Mackay was a Conservative. But he wisnae politically active as likes o' the elections and comin' down and goin' round the village and that sort o' thing.

He was a church elder. He went to Cockpen Church actually. Him and his wife very often used tae walk through the yard and walk over tae Cockpen, on the far side yonder, on a Sunday morning. And, as ah say, he was a keen Freemason.

I wouldn't believe that Mungo Mackay sent miners that were Catholics out to Rosewell and kept miners who were Protestants in and about Newtongrange, so as to divide the miners against each other. No, I couldn't believe that, because I worked here in Newtongrange and there were a lot of Catholics here. At the school, too, there were a lot o' Catholics in my class. In fact, there were no Catholic schools at that time. What happened was that we started the school at nine o'clock and the Catholics came in at half-past nine. It was the first half hour we got religious instruction at that time. And then the Lithuanians, they came across after the First World War, and they were all Catholics. I mean, it was a mixed bargain my class at the school. There wis as many Catholics as there were Protestants.

There might ha' been a little ill-feeling tae start wi' about the Lithuanians, because, let's face it, the Lithuanians were good workers, I mean, compared wi' some o' the men here they really were good workers. They stuck into their duties—which of course suited Mungo Mackay. But I can't recall my father or anybody else ever saying that was the main reason they were employed. They weren't regarded as blackleg labour. A lot o' them came before 1914, so they were well settled in by the time I was growing up.

In Mungo Mackay's days I worked all the time in either Lingerwood or Easthouses or Lady Victoria or the Bryans pit. The Bryans was a very old pit. There's a book written by Andra Clarke that tells ye the wages o' the men that worked in the Bryans and the women that worked in the Bryans carryin' the coal up in creels.[29] Well, the reason I worked at the Bryans—it must have been about 1929—was that the water coming off the Camp was beginning to rise, and it was tendin' to run down through the metals and into Easthouses. They were afraid it was goin' to the Lady Victoria, too. So by this time the water had risen half up the shaft at the Bryans. Eventually they couldn't cope with the amount of water that wis comin' down. So what happened wis that at that time ye could get down from the old limestone kilns at the far side, down into what they termed the day level, where the women yaist tae carry the coal up in creels. And what we did, we got quite a lot o' coal-cutter rubber trailing cables and pulled them down what they term the bourgate, down to the day level and connected them up wi' joint boxes, and then down to the foot of the shaft after that. Then the boilermakers and the blacksmiths dismantled a small pump at the workshops and made cases for conveyin' it across and down the pit. And there were a crowd o' labourers sent over from Easthouses tae help us. We finally got tae where the water was at the bottom o' the shaft. It was comin' up. Then we put the pump together and connected all the cables, got them up to the surface into the engine house and connected them up to the electricity there. Durin' the time that we were tryin' tae connect this up, of course, with the water bein' up there was no air circulation and the black damp was comin' in. Sweat was poorin' off us. We had no shirts on, it wis jist trousers on and boots, sweat was pourin' off us. Ah wis the apprentice at the time, and there wis two journeymen arguin'. One wanted tae go up, because ye couldnae get breath. The other yin wanted tae stay on and finish the job. Jist at that George Mackay comes doon. When he looks at the Davis safety lamp, he says, 'Come on, up out o' here, up out o' here!' And wis ah glad! Ah couldnae get breath. So we didnae get back down the pit that day. But what oo did do, they put up what they term a mid screen. They put canvas right down these posts, right along the length o' the bourgate. And we connected up a small fan on one side and it blew the gas down one side and up the other, which allowed us to return down to the other job o' buildin' the pump and connectin' up, which we duly managed to do. So within two or three days we managed to get that water down and out the shaft. That was the Bryans. But ah never came across anybody that had any conversation with iz regards the days o' serfdom in the Bryans.

When I started down Lingerwood in 1925 I was paid ten shillings a week. The second year I was paid twelve shillings, the third year sixteen shillings, the fourth year eighteen shillings. And when my time was out I was paid thirty-six shillings a week. At that time we worked under what they called a subsistence wage. Ye got sixpence extra on to make up your wage. But if ye worked overtime, that sixpence came off. We were workin' overtime for sixpence a shift less! That would be about 1930. I've seen me gettin' called out through the night, maybe a pump broken doon at the washer. Ye'd go oot and ye'd maybe have the job sorted in an hour. Ye were workin' for sixpence an hour, bein' hauled out yer bed and out there. That was usually in the small hours o' the mornin'.

When I started in Lingerwood at fourteen year old, after learnin' the sections I was what they termed a bell boy. They had bells right in the length o' the sections and at the engines. And after I learned the sections and knew my way about the pit I had to be up at four in the mornin' to get down the pit at five past five and be into the sections and test the bells, tae see that they were all right for the men comin' in tae start. They started at six o'clock in the mornin'. You finished about two o'clock in the afternoon, when you got up the pit. It wis a long day. At fourteen year old ye took it ill out, I can tell ye, gettin' up at four in the mornin'. Och, very often, ye'd jist fall asleep when ye got home.

Ye seen quite a lot o' fatalities in the pit in thae days. Tae a certain extent there was a certain lack o' care for the miners' safety. Ah believe the miners would be theirsels tae blame for some o' the things that happened—become careless to a certain extent. But then again of course sometimes the conditions were nae just o' the best tae work in in these days either. I used tae knock aboot wi' a boy that wis in ma class at the school. I was only aboot fifteen at the time and he was watchin' a door in one o' the sections. Full hutches broke away from the top, came down, smashed the door to bits, and—he was just comin' up tae see what was what—he was carried right out tae the main haulage in smithereens. Well, of course, that struck me hard because I used tae knock about wi' him regular, ye see. His funeral—well, at that time the drains at the Institute couldn't take all the water and it had been rainin' durin' the night before, heavens hard. It was a horse-drawn hearse and the water was up aboot two feet at the Institute. We couldnae walk. What'd we'd to do, we'd tae get up on tae the railings and cross the railings tae get past that part. Well, the hearse went through and we'd tae fall in at the other side.

I remember another time in Lingerwood. There wis a section that we had just about finished but this day it required an extension. So Andrew Garrett, the electrician, and I—I was sixteen, ye couldnae work overtime until ye were sixteen in these days—stayed on to do this extension. So we went in and commenced the extension cable. And here the last rake o' hutches goin' out caught the buildin' and closed the place. We couldnae get out that way. So we'd tae crawl up the wall. There was a narrow airway, oh, it wis jist aboot three feet high. I had a five-gallon oil can in front o' me that we'd filled up the switch wi'. We'd tae crawl about a hundred yards—tae me it seemed like a hundred mile—on oor stomach, pushin' the oil can. And if ye touched the sides sometimes it would come crumblin' in. Oh, it wis terrifyin' for me at sixteen year old! That was my first case o' that sort o' thing.

Mungo Mackay did have tale-bearers, he did have some o' these that carried tales up. They were men living in the village, they were known. Some were known anyway, and I expect that people would take care what they were saying to them that were known. None of my neighbours were tale-bearers.

I didnae see Mungo Mackay very often underground. The time I wis workin' he wis becomin' older and he would send his deputies down, if there was anything to be done. But he used tae have his deputies up and keep in touch wi' everything, ye see. And they kept him informed and of course he would give his verdict on what was to happen very often, without needin' to go down the pit.

Some o' the tale-bearers were ordinary miners, an occasional one or two, but he would get most of his information through the deputies.

The contractors, tae me, they used tae squeeze the men tae a certain extent. For example, when I was a laddie, I used tae go for my father's pay on a Saturday. He was contracted tae a man called John Pettigrew and ah wis sent for his pay packet. Very often his pay packet was £1.19.11½d. That wis tae keep ma father and mother and my sister and I. That would be just before the General Strike, just before ma father left the pits in 1925.

And in these days the miners had to buy their own tools. They'd tae buy their own explosives, their own drilling equipment. My father used tae keep his what they termed a rickety. It was a ratchet for boring with, and he used tae keep his squibs in the house sometimes. I remember he brought home a packet o' squibs that had got intae the water. He had dried them on the hob and put them into the dresser. So boy-like—I was at the school at the time—ah brought this packet o' squibs out. Ah put one on the hob and ah lit it and it shot across the whole length o' the kitchen and landed on the bedclothes. I had tae make a dive and hold on to it tae extinguish it! But, I mean tae say, in these days they had a' their own tools. I've got a shovel still, a No. 9 shovel, that ma father used down in Dalhousie section and it's as good today as it was in these days well ower sixty years ago. The shovels widnae last that now. I use it often.

Well, Mungo Mackay retired not very long before he died, and he was followed by his son George Mackay as manager. George was very exciteable. He was a very different kind o' man from his father. He hadnae the staid temperament that his father had. George died a few years ago.

One o' Mungo Mackay's other sons, Willie, was a farmer out at Selkirk, and his oldest girl was married on one o' the other pit men across this way. And then his other daughter Margaret, she's still livin' in Bonnyrigg. She's quite old now.

Mungo himself was quite tall, carried himself well—broad, straight, broad—and always had a stick, always had a stick. I remember his funeral right enough but no' a great deal about it. Ah don't remember o' goin' to it, tae tell ye the truth. Oh, well, I don't think all the blinds were drawn in the village!

ALEXANDER TRENCH

When ah left school at fourteen year old ah started in a little mine, a little pit it was, up at Vogrie in Gorebridge, owned by Gavin Paul and Company of Edinburgh. Ah worked there for maybe about two year, two year and a half. But the pit closed down for a little while and ah came down to Lady Victoria lookin' for a job.

We had to stand at the pit gate there in a queue lookin' for a job, because it was just very rare you got one. However, ah got a job with an old contractor on the nightshift, brushin', what we called brushin'. Now that would be in 1927, '28 maybe. And ah worked nightshift for a long time.

At that time we were on what we called the pool system, where all the money that was made, earned by the men on the day shift fillin' coal, that money had tae cover back shift, which were two men undercuttin' the coal, and six men on the night shift preparin' for the day shift the next day. The day shift were the only men that produced coal. And all that money was put intae a pool and it was divided up at the weekend between every man in the section. That was what we called the pool system. Ah got the chance to take a wage if ah wanted, but ah chose the pool system. So everybody workin' in that section at the time got that choice, tae work on for a wage or go into the pool.

Now ah would work under Mr Mungo Mackay for maybe just about two year—ah wisn't long—but ah still admire the work that that man planned out. There are three haulages in the Lady Victoria that are just like a memorial tae him. Haulages are roads made with arched girders that go right down into the coal. The coal's filled into tubs and these tubs are pulled up wi' a rope, and the empty tubs go down with the rope. So the haulages take the coal from the coal face to the pithead. Well, there are three in Lady Victoria and they're standing the same today as they did when Mr Mackay got these places developed maybe aboot, ah wid say, 1910 or 1912, something like that. They're really marvellous. And to look at that you must admire the man that had the technique at the back of all this. Mr Mackay was a very efficient man, very efficient. If he hadn't been efficient these places wouldn't ha' been standing the same as they are today. In fact, in later years they took away the haulage ropes and they put in a cable belt and they didn't need to alter one part o' that haulage way tae get this big cable belt laid in. That was one good thing about Mr Mackay—the way he planned the work.

It was never known in the Lady Victoria to have a strike. But we had one which lasted, if ah can remember, two weeks. It was Christmas week and New Year's week. And the strike was caused through the pit-bottomers wanting more money. Well, the union battled with Mr Mackay for more money and at the end Mr Mackay said, yes, he would give them more money—but on one condition: that he paid off all the old men that was sweepin' the pit bottom on night shift. They were cleanin' up with a brush and shovel, these old men, that's all they were fit to do. Mr Mackay had given them a job like this to keep them occupied, which I thought was very good. And he decided on this: the pit-bottomers would get more money and the old men would have to finish up. But the union agreed with Mr Mackay that he should just give the pit-bottomers as little as possible and keep the old men working in the pit-bottom, sweeping up. That wis the only strike ah can remember in Lady Victoria up till recent years where there are strikes everywhere, in every pit in Scotland and in Britain. So that was one good point about the Lady Victoria: when you worked there you got workin' every day in the week, no bother.

Well, in these days our union leaders wis Mr Pirie and Mr Rutherford. They were very efficient in lookin' into any complaint you had, because they were never away from that pit. They were up every afternoon—they had to work in the pit at that time—but after they come home they had to get cleaned and go up and battle it out with Mr Mackay about different things. They were very efficient these two union men, and as far as I know they got on very well with Mr Mackay in their arguments. They always came out, everybody was happy. Mr Mackay seen to it that there were no animosity caused, that the union really got on well, and Mr Mackay got on well with the union. It was the Midlothian Miners' Association at that time. Mr Pirie and Mr Rutherford were the two leadin' men for the Lady Victoria at that time.

Well, this village of Newtongrange in ma time when ah was just a young boy and started in the Lady Victoria, this village was really a model village. It was a model village all through Mr Mackay. He seen that it was a model village. At that time he decided to build bathrooms on to the houses, which they did do. Not long after they were built he decided that he could put in pithead baths, the first in Britain. The finest baths that was goin' tae be built was to be in Newtongrange for the pit. But at a miners' meetin' the men decided against it because they were already payin' a shillin' a week for the baths gettin' puttin' on to their house and Mr Mackay was goin' to charge, ah think it was, another shillin' for the pithead baths. So he got beat in that. But ah don't think he bothered very much about that because he had already put the bathrooms into the miners' houses.

In these days if you didn't dig your garden there was a man sent down to dig your garden for you and you paid for it. In a lot o' minin' or any other areas if the gardens have not been looked after, the village looks terrible. But it never looked terrible as far as Mr Mackay was concerned. He used to have a walk himself round the houses to see if the gardens were being looked after. But he had a policeman, the Lothian Coal Company policeman, and he reported all these things that wis goin' on in the village.

If things weren't right they were reported to Mr Mackay. And Mr Mackay sent for you, to 'go up the stair', as we called it. And when you knew you were goin' 'up the stair' it was no joke. You knew what you were goin' tae face. And you had to be clean, a collar and tie on, and go up and see Mr Mackay. Well, if you were down the pit and you were told you had to go up and see Mr Mackay, we knew when we come up the pit no' tae go and see Mr Mackay wi' our black face—there were no pithead baths in these days. We had to go home, get washed, and go up and see Mr Mackay maybe about three or four o'clock in the afternoon. But you knew not to go up with a dirty face, or dirty pit clothes on.

And he was very efficient and verra fair, ah'll say he was verra fair. He was very efficient in what he was saying an' askin' the questions: 'Why did you not do this? Why did . . .?' And you had to answer. If you didn't he fairly rapped you over the fingers for not doin' it properly.

Ah can't remember about a Green Table. He used to sit at a big table certainly. Ah couldn't tell you if it was a green table or not. The policeman was there most o' the time when you were goin' up, because there werenae jist one person told to go and see Mr Mackay—there were maybe about half-a-dozen, maybe a dozen. So he always had somebody there takin' evidence, you know.

Ah remember we got fined a pound for losing two grease

cups. Now grease cups were on machinery and they must have been lost some way, with the turning and the moving about as often. And we lost two o' them. So we were fined a pound. But that pound came off the pool. It wasn't one person that lost that pound, it come off the pool where there were maybe about twenty men included. But that was one of the things: if you did anything or you lost anything you had to pay for it.

Now being fined ten shillings in these days was a lot o' money. There no doubt it wis. It wis two days' wages, ten shillings in these days. All these fines, whenever he fined any person, well, you got the choice what hospital you sent them to. Most o' them were sent to Edinburgh Royal Infirmary. It wasn't the men who got fined made the decision, it was the miners' union agreed on this, that the fine went to 'ospitals.

PETER HERRIOT

Ah left the school when ah was fourteen in 1924 and ma first job in the pit was on the pithead, pickin' stones out o' the coal, at Smeaton colliery, also known as Dalkeith colliery. For that I was paid 1/11d. per day.

During that particular time the coal industry was in recession, the same as the rest o' industry. Not belongin' Newtongrange or any o' these minin' villages, of course, we didnae have the guarantee o' work, livin' in Dalkeith, that apparently they had at Newtongrange.

Although Dalkeith wis supposed to be a town and a burgh, the conditions were not much better—as a matter of fact, I believe in many instances they were even worse—than in some o' thae so-called minin' villages. Although I wasn't really livin' in a minin' village, aboot eighty per cent o' the population in Dalkeith did earn their livin' through the pits. We'd quite a variety o' small trades in Dalkeith—breweries, laundries, iron works, brass foundries, things like that. There were very, very few houses had more than one room to raise families in. Dalkeith was made in closes, ye ken, from the High Street tae the Back Street or St Andrew's Street. And there wis dozens and dozens o' families lived up these closes, where they had the one room and maybe a bed recess, and five and six o' a family. A water supply intae the houses wis only comin' in at that time. The bulk o' the closes in Dalkeith had maybe about one well where the people had to go and get water. The more advanced section had water in each individual house.

The lightin' wis in the main oil lamps. Although they did have a gas work and an electric works just had started, at that time they were bringin' over the electricity tae light the main roads, and they were daein' away wi' the gas. But ah still remember Auld Leerie goin' roond and lightin' the gas lamps up the closes. And it wis well intae the '30s before electricity was introduced as a form of lightin' in the houses and for cookin'.

Well, as I said, ma first job was on the pithead at Smeaton. Then I got a job in the drawin', which meant shovin' the empty hutches into the place where they were filled, fillin' them and shovin' them out. Now these hutches held about nine hundredweight o' coal. And they were on solid axles; there were no ball bearin's nor nothin' like that. They could be brute's work, because there wis many o' them used in what they cried snibble braes—which meant they were too steep for tae run normally: the man was never born that could hold it back. So what they did wis they put in two pieces o' wood—snibbles—in the spokes, to keep the wheels from runnin' round. Other occasions I had to put a piece o' sackcloth down in front tae haud them back. So you can imagine the type o' work that wid be. Plus the fact that efter a few months' runnin' ye got a' these flet bits on the wheels. So you try heavin' on the level, tae shove yin wi' bloody square wheels. Ye had somethin' tae do, for that's what it meant.

Smeaton or Dalkeith colliery was not as modern by any means tae the pits under the Lothian Coal Company. The Smeaton main haulage ways would be aboot three feet high. That wis the main haulage ways. There wisnae enough room tae swing a cat. If there wis an accident—a rope broke, or anything like that—there wis practically no place ye could go. That's how a lot o' the accidents did occur, because the ropes and that were not maintained as they should have been. The only time any place in the pit was maintained to the best of my knowledge was after an accident. Then everything that was required was suddenly brought in. These places only lasted for a certain time and then ye had to move on. I maybe spent two year at Smeaton colliery.[30] Then from there I went up to an auld pit by the name o' Cauld Hame, which is actually situated on the Pathhead road at Fordel. I had some experiences in Fordel. At the pithead there you could shout down to the bottom. They didnae bother wi' bells: they could shout doon to the pit-bottomer.

After spendin' a while at Fordel I went tae a stone mine in Gilmerton. That was drivin' a mine through the rock—very, very scientifically worked, too! This had been an old pit, the old Brosie. It had been worked about thirty or forty years previously. There were no plans or nothin' kept in these days o' the old workin's. So accordin' to the rules and regulations ye should have proceeded wi' a bore, which is borin' a hole away in front and puttin' a tube through, maybe twelve feet in front of you. So if you struck into old workin's the water would come through and would act as a warnin'. That was the theory. In practice, of course, they didnae work that way.

I remember this particular night—it illustrated tae me the power, the force, o' water. There wis only two o' us workin' in this particular section: the contractor—a chap wi' the name o' Eck Forrest—and maself, and ah wis only a laddie at the time, ah wis only a laddie. We had bored twenty-seven holes, which to the best o' ma knowledge was entirely against a' rules and regulations. And we had set them, charged them. This was for speed and everything. We lit them, a' twenty-seven, then out the road to have oor piece. All of a sudden we heard this rush of water and we got blewn through on to old workings. Before we could get very far we were up to this in water, hutches, and everything. We got out to the pit bottom eventually and was able to contact the windin' engineman, who took us to the surface. We were very, very fortunate that night tae get hame.

There were then nae modern baths nor nothin' like that. That meant I had a bike at that time. I was one o' the more better off, ye ken, than the ordinary miner: I could afford a bike. I was peyin' it off a bob a week. But that didna maitter. I still had it. But ye had tae cycle home frae Gilmerton tae Dalkeith, wi' jist your pit trousers on, a vest—and that wis you on a hard winter's day.

I never went back tae Gilmerton. I'd had enough o' that.

I also worked in the Moat colliery.[31] By the time I went tae the pits the pit ponies had been practically phased out and I had never came into contact with them. Till this particular day I was workin' in this section and I happened tae be last makin' ma way oot to the pit bottom. Unfortunately, when oo wis goin' through one o' the trap doors which controlled the air ma lamp blew oot. It wis total darkness. And here, I am—nae matches. And the nearest bloke, of course, he wis away in the distance. I couldna attract his attention at a'. The obvious thing tae dae was pit yer fit on the rail, pit yer hand on the wall, and try and guide yersel'. A' o' a sudden ah came tae something that wis hairy. Christ, ah thought it wis Auld Nick! Ah broke even time tae the pit bottom. Efterwards of course ah knew what ah'd touched had been a pit pony.

Frae the Moat ah got a job over in the Lady Victoria at Newtongrange. And that job was down the pit on what they termed the back brushin'. Now although ah had known about the Lothian Coal Company and about Mungie Mackay they were jist mainly stories, and this was the first time ah really had came intae more or less personal contact with them. I've got tae agree that he wis accepted as one o' the most brilliant minin' engineers in Scotland. But tae me as an individual, not stayin' in Newtongrange but havin' contacts wi' them, he was also a bit of a tyrant. He was actually one o' the remnants of the serf period. Up tae aboot 1750 or that if ye wis born in a minin' area ye belonged not to the human race but to the coalowner. And I believe there are records where about the last ones tae escape frae the Marquis o' Lothian's Coal Company were lodged in the jail at Dalkeith. It was about 1700-odds. But Mungo Mackay was carryin' on that idea.

Ah spent maybe six months at Lady Victoria and then ah got a job across in Easthouses on what they called pillarin' and steel-drawin', which is a form o' brushin'. That would be about 1927, 1928, jist roond aboot that time. Now at that time, although the unions werenae really encouraged they were still there. And of course anybody wi' political or union ideas werenae really encouraged either. In fact, at Newtongrange, if you wis inter-ested in the union or had any socialistic tendency, ye'd no bloody job. The bulk o' them that were socialists in Newtongrange had tae do it under cover. They'd join up in Dalkeith, which I believe was the second place in Midlothian tae form a Labour Party—Musselburgh was the first. Of course, there wis other socialist organisations preceded that—the Independent Labour Party and the Social Democratic Federation, that kind o' thing.[32]

Now there wis quite a few o' us—Mungie Mackay not havin' the same hold on us as what he had on more or less what we used tae term the natives—had a wee bit more independence, at least in ideas. And we were advocatin' against the contractor system at that time. We were agita-tin' for what they termed penny aboot.

The contractin' system—and the system that ah worked in wis generally contractors—wis a system whereby they went to an individual and they said, 'You're a contractor. We'll gie you so much a ton.' He in turn did get as much work for the cheapest labour. Well, it wis quite an advantageous way o' runnin' any type o' business, especially the coal industry at that time. It meant that a man was putten in charge o' a section. Now he either had so much per ton or, depending on the types of work, they were paid so much per lamp or per man. Then the contractor decided what the wage would be. And in many cases it meant of course that if the contractor had a considerable number of men working with him he had quite a substantial income. Although the average wage in Newtongrange was a wee bit lower than what could be earned in other outside collieries. The contractin' system of course was not only a way of bein' more efficient in the workin' but it also helped Mungie Mackay tae keep the control over the people, because these contractors had tae report back tae Mungie Mackay not only on the working o' their section, or explain why there wis deficiencies—say, not sufficient production—but also to let him know the type o' individual and what they were gettin' up tae. Many a fellae didnae turn oot tae his work for some reason and the contractor wisnae satisfied wi' the explanation. So Mungie Mackay, of course, took over and he got an explanation o' some kind. It meant that the bloke was fined of course. That wis the normal procedure.

Now there wis many o' these contractors had so many men workin' wi' them that they actually didnae require to go doon the pit at all. All they had to do wis to put somebody, a chargehand, in and then they drew the money. It wis a very, very good system if you happened to be a contractor. But ah'm rather afraid that that wis no' the kind o' system that ah personally agreed wi'.

So, as ah say, we were agitatin' for penny aboot. Of course, if ah wis usin' the correct phraseology it would be 'penny about'—which simply meant this, that there was a price given for the production of the coal and for the brushin' and the pan-shiftin'. So instead o' that money goin' tae one contractor and he paid ye a wage, it simply meant that ye had one leadin' man who had sixpence a day above the rest of ye. The rest was equally shared amongst you. The colliers had so much for producin' the coal—I think it was about 11½d. a ton at that time. We had sixpence a fathom for the brushin', and the panshifters of course they were paid what was termed the average wage—which meant the average of what the rest o' the colliery were bein' paid.

Now Mungie Mackay had got tae hear that we were agitatin' for penny aboot. And the section that I wis employed in wis a' summonsed tae appear in front o' this Green Table. We wis summonsed for disciplinary action, as we had been workin' contrairy tae the ideas acceptable tae Mungie and underminin' his establishment.

So we all appeared there up in the Lady Victoria. Ee were taken intae this big room, the great big table, Mungie sittin' at one side and the constable at the other. And oo got a lecture, of course, aboot this Bolsheev-ikism and underminin' society! And oo wis told that it wis unfortunate for us but that he wid be dispensin' wi' oor services—no' because of our views but because the place that we were workin' in wis bein' closed, it wis uneconomical. So that wis ma first experience o' that. It wis obvious of course what the real reason wis.

Well, ah found on two occasions at least—one was in the Lady Victoria and one was in Easthouses—because o' ma political allegiance ah couldnae get a job. Ah wis an undesirable. And ye know that spread right through the pits. Trade unionism wis only in its infancy. And to be a trade unionist— if you became a leader, ye had no job either. And that applied to all the collieries in the district. To overcome that, of course, what they had to do wis appoint minin' inspectors and checkweighmen. That wis only so as that they could have a livin' wage. And that wis the way they existed. It was founded in the district when they couldnae get a job in any colliery at a'.

Now Mungie Mackay had many virtues and many sins. I

don't think there's anybody would attempt to take away from the man's ability as a minin' engineer. As a matter of fact, it's only two or three years ago ah went down one o' the most modern collieries in Scotland, and ah can truthfully say that the roads system and the haulage system werenae much in advance o' what they had in the Lady Victoria. See, he had the foresight tae see that it would be beneficial tae his industry tae have good lines o' communication. And he certainly did provide that, although there wis many other things he maybe jist went a wee bit too far on – like husbands and wives fa'in' oot, which is not an uncommon thing. And any reports—they had tae appear in front o' Mungie. They were fined. You didn't pay the fine—it was subtracted from your pay sort o' automatically. And then of course that wis donated tae charity—in the main, the Edinburgh Royal Infirmary. Eventually, of course, even the Infirmary, when they heard about how the money was accumulated, they refused tae take it.

Bear in mind this, that although the people in Newtongrange had always a house and a job, it wis only at the discretion o' Mungie. You do anything which he felt was detrimental to him or to the Lothian Coal Company and then you were in trouble. Because he had this great hold on ye. Not only did ee lose yer job—you lost, equally important, a roof over your head. And so there wisnae too many prepared tae take that.

The thing that surprised me of course was that the rebel spirit in Newtongrange wisnae completely destroyed, although it had to seek other outlets. One o' the main things that ah personally know of wis when they started the Labour Party in Dalkeith. Some o' our most prominent and able members came from the village o' Newtongrange. One o' the ablest men ever it's been ma privilege tae know, and one o' the most brilliant orators ever ah knew, wis a chap by the name o' Andy Anderson. Now he couldnae be employed locally but eventually he wis fortunate enough in gettin' a job wi' the Co-operative Society as an insurance agent. And he had tae do most o' his work on behalf o' the minin' community and the conditions o' the people in Newton-grange, from the outside angle.[33]

And there wis many, many others prominent, of course, who had to do likewise. They had to leave the village and work on the outside. So that was really the worst o' it.

LEWIS MORRISON

I was born in Newtongrange in 1915. My father was a
Dalkeith man and he was in the pits. He took a tumour in
the brain and he died, a young man, when I was five. I canna
remember a lot about him. As I say, we had a wee bit o' a
struggle. My mother, she had three others, and there was one
on the way. I was the oldest o' the five. My mother was a
Newtongrange woman. She got a job cleanin' the school.
Eventually we went tae live wi' ma granny, her mother. And
they brought us up and ma mother worked in the school.

I went tae Newbattle School and I was dux o' the school.
Mrs Mungo Mackay always presented the dux medal. And
my mother was there, and she told ma mother tae send me up
tae see Mr Mackay. Well, I had thought maybe on clerical
lines. I didnae want tae be a miner, I didnae want tae be a
miner. There were nothing else for us in these days. I thought
maybe I would get a job in the workshops or maybe be a
clerk.

I left the school on the Friday and they told me tae come up
on the Monday mornin'. I went up to Mungo Mackay's
house. I cannae remember the interview but he wis very nice. I
don't know if he kept his eye on the duxes at the school. I
don't know o' any other one that wis there, I was the only one
I know of. I think it wis jist Mrs Mackay maybe just took a
likin' tae me or to the looks o' me. I don't know, but
something like that. Mungo Mackay thought a lot o' her,
you know. She was a nice person, a gem o' a woman.

I went tae the office after that. Talk about the Green Table! A bell underneath it: one ring for the apprentice, two for the boss. So he rung two and John Terris, the chief surveyor, came in and he jist introduces me and tells him: 'Take him through and start him.' I didnae know what a surveyor was at that time. But he couldnae have picked it better for me. I liked my work, I really enjoyed it.

Ah liked Mungo Mackay, of course. I'm no' one o' the ones that's goin' tae talk against him. He wis good tae me. Mrs Mackay always asked hoo ah wis gettin' on. And I think he just sort o' kept a wee bit eye on me. He took quite a fatherly interest in me, oh, he definitely did.

What ah did at first, well, in these days there wis always a lot o' clerical work tae be done in the survey office, and I did a lot o' clerical work. The new start always got the clerk's job before he started the surveying at all. He was the boy, and when the button under the Green Table went it was one ring for the boy, two rings for the boss, Mr Terris. And when that button went I used tae go hoppin' along, jist along the corridor. Our room was up the stair, but jist along the corridor from Mungo Mackay's. Ah did his messages and, ach, I did everythin'—down into his accounts, and runnin' across maybe tae take somebody tae any o' the various bosses, jist anythin', jist office laddie.

In the surveyors' office there wis a' the surveyors. But they were never called in question. It wis the boss, Mr Terris, or the youngest one, me. There were the boss, there was a qualified assistant, and there may have been another qualified assistant, maybe about five or six apprentices. As I say, the youngest apprentice always did this spell o' clerkin' before he stepped up tae the main room.

Ye had tae go tae evening classes, oh, aye, ye had tae go. Mungo Mackay widnae have had any time for ye if ye didnae go. There were no day release. Surveying classes were generally held at night and the mining classes on a Saturday afternoon. And it was Saturday afternoon frae four tae seven. We had tae give up a' the football tae go. Ye finished work at one on a Saturday, it wis a five-and-a-half day week. Then ye had tae go to Edinburgh tae Heriot Watt College, frae four tae seven. Ye had tae leave Newtongrange about three o'clock. Oh, Mungo Mackay widnae have had any time for ye if ye hadnae gone.

Well, I qualified, I was twenty-one when I qualified and I started when I was fourteen. So that was seven years I went to classes. Oh, we didnae go every Saturday afternoon because it was, I think a five-year course. Then on the weekdays it wis a couple o' nights or a night a week. In addition to that I used to take a correspondence course and I did a lot in the house. I worked hard tae get my ticket.

In the office it was from nine tae five and frae nine tae one on a Saturday. And then, of course, when I say 'in the office' that wis your hours, but we were underground as well. We done a lot o' underground. We were up and down quite a lot in the three pits—the Lady Victoria, Lingerwood and East-houses. We did the three o' them.

I started wi' ten bob a week. Then I got half a croon o' a rise every year. I had thirty bob when I qualified. Then I got £1 o' a rise. That was £2.10.0d. I was twenty-one then. I was goin' wi' ma wife at that time. I went away and I got another job. I think it was the Wemyss Coal Company in Fife. Mungo Mackay called me in and he telt me he didnae want me tae go. And he gave me £3.15.0d. That was what I had when I got married, £3.15.0d! That was above the average for a mining surveyor. I'd say an average at that time would probably be about £3 a week—ten bob a shift. That would be in 1939–40. So I never went tae the Wemyss Coal Company. I jist stayed at Newtongrange. I didnae want tae go tae Fife anyway. I was hopin', I was hopin'—and he did, so . . . I've always worked and I've always lived here in Newtongrange.

I worked wi Mungo Mackay for roughly ten years. Ah started in 1929 and he died in 1939. He was a great minin' engineer. Some o' the best roads in that pit were still the roads that they made even long after the Lady Victoria was nationalised. The best roads in the pit were the roads that he supervised. He was a good minin' engineer. There is no doubt about that.

He was tall, oh, he was tall, and he was a wise-like man, oh, God, aye. Erect, and he was quite a nice lookin' man, really. I would say he was a striking looking man, the type o' man ye'd look at and say, 'Oh, that's the boss, a'right.' He had an air o' authority.

He was abrupt, aye, he wis abrupt. But he had his good points and a'. In the office it wis jist a long corridor. We were at this end, he was at that end. Now in between that was the stairs. Now ninety-nine times out o' a hundred he came along and went doon the stairs. But the hundredth time he came through to our office. He never came through withoot coughin'. I've never known him tae come in withoot aaagghh, aaagghh, ken—clearin' his throat. I think he did it on purpose, jist tae say: 'Here I'm comin'. You'd better sit up!' He could stand at the door and look round and then talk to Terris, the boss. There was a feelin' when he appeared that ye sat up and got crackin'. But at the same time I widnae say that any o' us were frightened for him. We were maybe a wee bit in awe. But they took him, they just took him—he never was bad to the surveyors, ye see.

The thing was the surveyors, there were a very, very short life. Ye served your apprenticeship, sat your examinations, qualified, and then ye were generally away. There was very few, very few qualified men left, because they a' went into mining or a' went into building or a' went into something else. They didn't stay long as soon as they qualified. They wanted out. Some o' them didnae want tae be in the pit a' the time. I was one o' the few that stayed. They were intent on qualifying and getting away. So they werenae all that bothered. They knew they werenae going tae be there for life, werenae going tae be tied tae the job. There was more an independent spirit among the surveyors than among the miners, because they wid find it more difficult to get other jobs. The surveyors never did anything wrong and, as I say, I think Mungo Mackay looked on the surveyors as his boys. They were his boys. When he wanted anything it was the surveyors' room he came into. Because he was a minin' engineer himself he would probably feel closer in some ways to the surveyors. Well, I'm not going to say he had nothing to do with the clerical department, which was downstairs. There were no doubt he would be keeping his eye on them as well! But he never had anythin' to do wi' the clerical staff. It was the minin' staff or the engineers, the electricians—we were his boys, no doubt about that. His attitude to the clerical staff was quite different.

I think the ordinary miner—it's no' easy tae say this—but if he was a good miner, a good worker, he never had any bother wi' Mungo Mackay. But if he was one o' the rebels and didnae want tae work, then Mungo Mackay had no time for him. I mean, the people who didnae like him—I suppose you've heard a lot about that. But they're the type. Now take the people who co-operated wi' him and did what he wanted ye tae dae, ye never had any problem. The majority of the Newtongrange miners were really quite passive. They accepted everything. They had been brought up wi' it.

There were only one union man here. John Rutherford wi' the game leg, he was the union man. And I think they co-operated very well, him and Mungo Mackay. I think they got on very well. I think John widnae dae anythin' tae upset

Mackay! John was anything but a militant, anything but. It was only after nationalisation that ye got the militants comin' in.

But I think it's a' true a' this stories aboot puttin' people out their hooses and a' this sort o' thing, probably it is true, though I couldnae give ye any specific cases. But it probably is true. I have no doubt he would tell a man if he wisnae workin' that he would take him out o' his house. Or maybe if his son wouldnae go to the pit. I think he was capable o' doin' that. Ah heard jist rumours, the same as everybody else.

I really think—though again I have no proof—I think people carried stories. He had story-tellers, he had people in the village who carried everything up to him. I believe that, too, yes, I believe that, too. I remember once, he sent me doon tae the Post Office in the village tae pay an account. I smoked, I had started smokin' at that time, an' unconsciously ah must have lit up a cigarette. When ah went back up tae the office he called me in. He says, tappin' the table: 'You were smokin'.' Somebody must have told him even before I went back to the office. I got a long lecture. He didnae give me a row for smokin', he gave me a lecture. He said I widnae grow—but I was growing big. I'm aboot five foot eleven! But ah liked him. He was good to me.

I was never there when he was dealin' wi' anybody at the Green Table. That wasn't part o' my business. The Green Table wis a big table, a green-top table. I think possibly it would maybe be six to eight feet, four feet wide. I don't think it would be any bigger. Dinnae get the wrong impression that it wis the width o' the room! But it wis big enough for havin' meetings and men sittin' roond it. It wis topped wi' green baize stuff like a card table. Mungo Mackay always sat facin' the door.

Frank Taylor, the village policeman, was generally there. He was employed by the Constabulary and seconded to the colliery. I would think the colliery would pay his wages, part o' them anyway. He was the one that got the blame o' tellin' stories. He stayed in the village, up in Lothian Terrace. I lived there myself. I quite liked Frank. He's dead long syne. He had a daughter ages wi' me. He was a constable but he wasnae the only village policeman, there were three that ah know of. But he was the colliery policeman. He was the one that always sat in at the Green Table.

I knew they got fined. Mungo Mackay used tae fine them and send it to the Infirmary. I knew that. There wis always people waitin', ye could see them in the corridor. Oh, I'm no' gaun tae say there wis a queue but there wis always one or two standin' aboot waitin'. I don't know what it was for: no' jist in trouble—maybe they would have to see him about anything. I mean, everybody that wis standin' in the corridor wisnae in trouble. I think mysel' he was the type o' man that if ye went up tae see him, well, wi' a legitimate case he would listen tae ye. I suppose you had tae be ready tae stand up for yoursel'.

I never had interviews wi' him like that. Ye see, I dealt wi' my own boss for time off and increases. But once I got a row wi' Mungo Mackay. I cannae mind what it wis but I got a row. I got a row for something and I didnae know whether tae greet or laugh—and I laughed! Oh, I was in trouble then, right enough! Oh, what I got! Oh, he was goin' tae send me hame! He didnae do it and I don't think he would have. But he was lettin' me know, like. Oh, I didnae know whether tae cry or laugh—and I laughed. I cannae mind what it wis. He gave me an awfy tellin' off about something.

He used tae walk doon the village wi' his stick. He always had a walking stick. He knew everything that was going on. People would go up and tell him and if there were anybody no' doin' their garden ye can rest assured he would know who it was. I mean, I wisnae aware that he went up and looked at the gardens but ah wouldnae be surprised. He would tell them—he would send for them and tell them tae get their garden done, or else. I don't know what 'or else' would mean, but he could maybe threaten them—make them do it onyway!

It was a big village, Newtongrange, in fact, about the biggest coal-mining village in Scotland. The Lothian Coal Company built different kinds o' houses in it. There was Lothian Terrace, up by Lingerwood Farm yonder. Lothian Terrace is a row of twenty-four houses, double-storey. That's where I stayed until very recently. They were officials' houses. They were five-apartment. These ones up at the Saughs—that wis the officials' houses. The chief surveyor and everybody lived in that row. We were a wee group on our own, separated from the ordinary miners. The contractors jist lived in the village. They didn't live in separate streets, but they would get a good house. They would be looked on quite favourably. They were a'—you know, that's what I mean about the favoured few. They probably thought Mackay was great. The officials got bigger houses—five-apartments—but the rest o' the houses, I think if they were different categories it was jist because o' the age o' the houses and the size o' the family. For instance, Ninth Street, that's four-apartments. That's for the larger families. It had nothing to do wi' your place in the hierarchy. It's jist that when they were built, well, frae First Street to Sixth Street there were no bathrooms or anything. They were a' put in later. But frae Sixth Street and right along tae Tenth Street, they were a' new houses. They were built after the First War. I mind o' them bein' built. My mother went into Ninth Street new and I was fourteen, so that wis jist when I started in the pits—1929. And then Galadale: I went into that when I was married, new! Of course, I got a house, tae. I was one o' the favoured few. I went into Galadale—well, I was married in '40, and that was when Galadale was built. So, as I say, if the houses are different it's because o' age rather than any other reason. Ninth Street, as I say, they're four-apartments. They'd be built for the families. There would be maybe forty or fifty years between the earliest streets and the later ones.

I cannae really remember it but I know that there was quite a big influx o' people frae the west o' Scotland intae Newtongrange. The pits were bein' worked out through in the west. They used tae say they were frae 'through yonner.' This was the expression. They could be in Newtongrange a' their life and never be accepted because they came frae 'through yonner'! There wis a lot but individually I couldnae name them. After the 1926 General Strike, that's the time o' the recession, there were a lot of people came. And I suppose they were jist like the locals. If they were good men, good workers, they would get on OK. And if they werenae, if they were the rebellious type, they wouldnae get on. Ye had tae do as ye were telt.

We a' went tae Newbattle School, Catholics or Protestants. Oo a' went tae the school thegither. There wisnae this bigotry that there is now. Oh, there was a big chapel in Rosewell. Oh, aye, Rosewell wis known as Little Ireland. That's where a' the Catholics were put, at Rosewell. But Mungo Mackay at that time didnae have anything to do wi' it. It wis Mr Hood that looked after Rosewell. Hood was the General Manager before Mungo. Mungo took over Rosewell eventually, and I think that possibly Mungo inherited the fact there were so many Catholics at Rosewell, rather than had anything to do wi' it. The Catholics and the Irish who came looking for work a' settled in Rosewell. Well, ah don't know if they were sent there. They seemed tae a' land there anyway. I never heard o' Mungo Mackay bein' sectarian. As I say, we all went to the school together and half o' the laddies I played aboot wi' were Catholics. We never thought anything aboot it. Ah never ever, never was aware that in the Lothian Coal Company people maybe didnae get promoted because they were Catholics.

The Lithuanians, well, they were Poles. But these Poles were a' good workers. They were a' thought a lot o', the Poles. They were Catholics but they a' got hooses and they a' got jobs. By the time I started work they were well intae the second generation. Ye see, their families were goin' tae school wi' me. They were second generation. Some o' them had changed their Lithuanian names. For instance, I know one chap, his name was Johnny Rasciewic when I was at the school. Now he cries hissel Johnny Rose.

Oh, the Lithuanians were heavy drinkers. I think it was a' Saturday night stuff. When they were drunk a few o' them got involved in fights. I don't think it wis anything else other than drink! That's my recollection anyway.

The Dean Tavern, of course, was run by a committee, just the same as it is now. Mr Mackay would be head, of course. It was the Lothian Coal Company, well, their money put it there. And although it was a committee formed wi' local people the union people—John Rutherford—would be on it and Mackay would be on it, J.C. Murray, the Company secretary, would be on it.[34] But it wis run for the benefit o' the village. And they gave away a lot o' money in these days. The Dean Tavern money built the bowling green. I've an idea they built the band hall as well, but I'm not sure about that one. The Dean would do their bit to keep the village band up. You see, a' that was run by the Dean Tavern.

And the village band was the Newtongrange Colliery Band. So Mungo Mackay would have a part in that too! If they wanted anything—up and saw Mungo! The brass band had a uniform. They had a pipe band as well. The pipe band wore kilts. And then what they did was they brought the band-master, when I was a kid, they brought him frae the west somewhere and gave him a job as blacksmith in the colliery. It wis a' tied up wi' the colliery. Football—the colliery built the Newtongrange Star football pitch. It wis a' colliery or the Dean. And the Dean was the colliery, ye see, the biggest part o' it anyway.

Mungo Mackay was a great Masonic man. His photograph's hingin' on a' the wa's in the Masons'. I would agree wi' sayin' that if you were in the Masons it helped. Oh, they were looked on quite favourably. I would say that was one way o' risin' in the Company. And, oh, the church, too, oh, the church, too: the Masons and the church. The clerical side o' the Company was the church one. Mr Murray, he was the secretary o' the Company, he was a church man and an elder, too. It was the United Free then, the bottom church. But Mr Mackay was the Masons, that was the difference. If you went to the church or the Masons you had a chance, aye, o' risin' in the Company. And if ye didnae go to the church or the Masons, well, ye maybe no' hae very much chance! It took a bit longer! Ye got on in the Clerical Department through the church and ye'd probably get on in the Management Department throught the Masons. I was a Mason but I was never a practisin' Mason. It never did anything for me. I dinnae mean, when I say that, I dinna mean that it didnae do anything for me money-wise or job-wise. It jist didnae dae anythin' for me. I was never interested in it. I was never active in it.

I never heard o' Mungo Mackay havin' any political activity. I've no doubt he would be a diehard Tory. But I've never heard o' him bein' politically active. I never knew him havin' any political interests. His interest was his pit. He could go oot there at night and walk round the pit, see thae people who were on backshift, talk to them. He wis quite a hard-workin' man. I cannae ever recollect him havin' a holiday. He was always there. I think he would have been ill away frae the place.

Oh, he enjoyed good health. Then he took a heart attack.

Oh, aye, he was in good health up to that. I mean, he was beginnin' tae get on in years at that time.

I attended his funeral, oh, a big turn-out. It was the one and only time I ever wore a bowler hat! I borrowed it specially, I got it frae somebody. Everybody wore bowler hats in these days at funerals. The body lay at Lingerwood House and then he was buried in Newbattle cemetery. There was a procession but I cannae mind if it was a horse-drawn hearse. I think it was a motor and I think we a' jist waited at the churchyard. We didnae march at the back o' it, I don't think so anyway. There were a big crowd, a big funeral. He was well known in the minin' industry. I wid think the colliery would close that day, but I jist cannae remember. Aye, that was the one and only time I ever had a bowler hat on!

After he died the village changed. There wisnae the discipline. His son George Mackay followed him as General Manager. And he wasnae interested, really he wasnae interested in the pit. And there were a bloke called John Stewart, he came as assistant to George Mackay. And he sort of gradually took over and he became the one. And then along comes nationalisation. Now George still got the job, what they cried sub-area General Manager. But he didnae last long, he didnae last long. He wasnae so devoted. They got him into a safety job or something and got another man in his place. He wasnae really interested in mining, I don't think. I think he wanted tae be a farmer. He married a farmer's daughter from D'Arcy. Anyhow that wis George.

Then Mungo Mackay had another son, Eric. Eric was in the navy, I think it was the Royal Navy. And he had another son, Wullie. He was a farmer. Wullie wasnae very strong. He died comparatively young. Then Mungo had two daughters. One wis Margaret. I cannae remember the other one's name. They jist married locally. But Mungo Mackay had a family of five—five I know of anyway. They were older than me.

When Mungo spoke he tried tae talk English but, I mean, he didnae put anything on. He didnae have a strong West o' Scotland accent. He belonged tae Ayrshire but I widnae say that he had a strong Ayrshire accent. Oh, he'd been through here at Newtongrange frae an early age. Ach, I liked him anyway, and he was good tae me.

TOMMY THOMSON

When ma father married ma mother ma father was a miner and ma mother wis a master builder's daughter. And Mr Mackay was very reluctant to learn that ma grandfather had allowed his daughter tae marry a miner. And this was impressed upon me right from ah wis young.

I was born in 1903 and I met Mr Mackay when I was only a boy, because my grandfather was the ganger to Thomas Campsie and he was building the third phase in the village. It incorporated The Square and surroundings, and he was responsible for taking down the Black Wood. He was also responsible for building Deanpark. The one-storey houses cost £65 to build. The double-storey houses on the main street were built for £92.10.0d. When they were altered and the miners got in the benefits of up-to-date facilities, the extensions were made on these houses for £15.

My father was a church officer and I came in contact with different members of Mungo Mackay's family as a boy, as his eldest daughter took an interest in the children in the village.

Well, I was workin' in Gilmerton pit in 1935–36 and when ah went back then to the Lothian Coal Company ah went back with great praise from the Divisional Inspector o' Mines, Mr Foster, and ah went back with great praise from J.R. Wilson.[35] And the first thing that ah got after ah wis four days started in the Lady Victoria wis, 'Ye've tae come up the stair at half-past three.' Well, in those days, when the house and the job went thegither, ye knew what you were in for.

So of course I went up this day and Mr Mackay was sittin'
on the Green Table, swingin' his legs. That wis something
new. When you went in tae see old Mungie, the policeman
was standin' there, Mungo was in the chair, the manager was
here, the undermanager was here, and you'd tae stand wi'
your cap in your hand. But he was only himself this day.
'Tom,' he said, 'the manager in Lingerwood's had an accident.' He said, 'Ah've sent for you because,' he said, 'ah want
tae know about the alterations you made in the Gilmerton
pit.'

'Well,' I said, 'to be quite frank with you,' I said, 'I must
thank ma father because he was the most greetin'-faced man
ah ever worked with, ma own father. It was for ma benefit
and,' ah says, 'ah must thank ma father and ah must thank
you,' ah says, 'for the experience that ah got here. And, 'ah
said, 'that wis the reason that ah got the build up both from
Mr Wilson and from Mr Foster.'

'Ah' he said, 'ah want you to go as an oversman into the old
pit—Lingerwood.' I said, 'Well,' I said, 'MrMackay, I'll have
to think it over.' 'Now, Tom,' he said, 'you're goin' into that
pit as oversman on one condition.' I said, 'What's that?' He
says: 'That you come and tell me everything that's goin' on.'
'Well,' I said, 'you're askin' the wrong person tae come and
tell you everything that's goin' on.' 'Now,' he says, 'let me be
fair with you.' He says, 'You see the whole of the oversmen I
have appointed,' he says, 'in all the three pits?' I said, 'Yes.'
'Well,' he says, 'they've appointed themselves. They come
carryin' the tale to me.' He says, 'Ah know ninety per cent of
what's goin' on in the collieries.' He says, 'That's how things
are and,' he says, 'ah want tae appoint you, because ah've
been hearing good reports about you.' He said, 'Ah've never
yet appointed an oversman that's never come to me without
tellin' the tale. So,' he says, 'ah want to have a check on
everything that's in Lingerwood.' 'Well, Mr Mackay,' ah

said, 'if that's the case you're no' gettin' me.' He said, 'Come on, now, away you go home and think it over for a fortnight.' But ah never would take the oversman's job.

Now ah mentioned the policeman, who was employed by the colliery. In those days Arniston Coal Company had a policeman tae. And Niddrie and Benhar Coal Company had a policeman. Now Billy Ritchie, the Rangers goalkeeper, was born in Nitten in the policeman's house.[36] And when his father was transferred through here from West Lothian his next-door neighbour, who was the senior policeman, told him: 'In this village there's a system. They don't want to see any person bein' taken into the Sheriff Court if it can be avoided.' The policemen worked with the colliery policeman. Mungo Mackay used to fine the miners—in agreement with the Coal Mines Regulations. If you did something in the pit you could pay a fine as agreed upon by Mr Mackay, or you could go to court. That's in the Coal Mines Regulations and the village just worked on that basis, on that principle. And there's many a chap, believe me, who's been fined by Mungie Mackay who would have been getting thirty or sixty days if he'd gone tae the court. Now years and years ago, it was one of the agreements with the Lothian Coal Company that you paid a penny a week for the Royal Infirmary. And all fines that Mr Mackay imposed, whether it be for something in the village or something in the colliery, the money went to the Edinburgh Royal Infirmary. That happened in all the pits—you'd tae name a charity. If you were fined for a misdemeanour, you named a charity—Salvation Army, Infirmary . . .

Well, Mungie Mackay—and ah say it wi' all sincerity—was the greatest civil engineer that was in this district. And the reason that he was was simply because he grew with the job. He knew his work. He left plans in this area to keep the Lothian Coal Company solvent for 200 years. Mungo Mackay was out and out one of the most outstanding mining engineers that ever was in Scotland.

When Mr Hamilton, the manager there, died Mungo Mackay took over Polton pit and Rosewell, better known as Whitehill. And his biggest difficulty was the rebuilding of Polton pit bottom. It was a wet pit and the first thing that Mungo Mackay did was that he hired a marine pump from Leith to put in the shaft. But with them disturbing the metals the water came rushing in and for days they couldn't work. The girders had in fact to be put very close.

Mungo Mackay also had the Lady Victoria, Lingerwood—the old pit—and Easthouses. And one thing that he did: every shaft should have had an out-going shaft. But there were only three shafts in this district. And when the big pit was sunk at Lady Victoria the first thing that he did was draw up a drift from the Dixon shaft to the Lady. It meant that, with the intentions of turning across four different seams of coal, he only managed to get three. The first seam that he struck was the cannel coal—better known in this district as the Dalhousie dook. Then they sunk further down and went on to the splint. And then they drove a long mine which meant that there had to be a long return shaft or dook or incline for the main splint dook. He came across and then he turned into the Carrington area. That allowed him not only to take the cannel coal there but the kail blades and the grade seam. The fourth seam that he wished to go into was sunk—and they were the four seams.

He was a man for output. My grandfather had built the Lady Victoria pit bottom, which was something like the Waverley Station. At the beginning of Mungo's time there were heavy horses used for drawing the tubs into the pit bottom to be loaded. But the next thing that he wanted was a quick returnin' loader. He had a cage made where both decks could be filled. The double-deck cage lifted eight ton o' coal at a time. In fact, actual weight of the load from the pit bottom goin' to the surface was thirty tons. The shaft was twenty feet wide and there were no rail guides in it. It was a rope, and when the cage was in mid-shaft the ropes began to swing. So Mr Mackay struck on the idea that the weights at the end of each rope would be different. When the cages passing in mid-shaft run at a speed of thirty-two miles an hour they just missed one another sometimes by less than two inches.

They were winding in that shaft in 1903, before Mungo Mackay was properly the manager, when the teakwood on the brakes of the winding engine started to burn and both cages dropped to the bottom of the shaft. Luckily enough, there were nobody hurt. But it meant that they had to go back down the Dixon shaft and along the mine, and it was 1904 before they got things properly seen to.

It was 1906 when the Lady Victoria went into full production. The intention was workin' only four seams. But the first thing that they did was to make the main item safety, and everyone was encouraged that safety would come before output. In those days the miners had to go into the magazine for their explosives. And they brought it home in a 14lb box. That was bobbinite, numbers 1 and 2. Every miner had to go to the chemist to buy sulphur. He mixed the sulphur in a basin, and the sheets of the *Evenin' News* were taken and put in and hung up in their back kitchens to dry. Then they were folded up. And when the miner had bored the hole in the coal he inserted this reel or turn of bobbinite, stuck in his piece of paper which had been tightly folded, then put a light to it. That's how they fired their coal in those days.

In 1912 output wasn't what they expected, so Mungie Mackay went out to have the long-wall working. For the lower seams it was to be a shaker conveyor, and for the higher seams Blacket conveyors. After these were put in one of the pits—the old pit, Lingerwood—the men were producing coal at 11d. per ton. And everything in the Lothian Coal Company collieries from then seemed to come away with larger increases of output. In fact, in 1914 the Lady Victoria supplied practically the whole of the British navy with hard coal. One contractor at that time who had always the habit of shouting to his men: 'Come on, lads! Jellicoe's needin' coal!' won for himself the name o' Jellicoe Smith.[37]

As Mr Mackay received further promotion at the Lothian Coal Company, he became too immersed in profit. There was one day I had to go 'up the stair' for he wanted to see me about an airway being built up. He was in a state that day because a young lad had went round the [winding] drum in the old pit and had been killed. The Lothian Coal Company were fined for that. When ah went in before the Green Table Mr Mackay was sittin' at the back o' the table, the manager was standing at one side, and Frank Taylor, the policeman, at the other. Ah said: 'Mr Mackay, there's one thing about you.' He says, 'What's that, Tom?' Ah says: 'Ye can tell everybody's bad points but ye cannae tell many good ones.' He says, 'Have you got any good points?' Ah says, 'Yes.' He says, 'That'll do from you. Out the door.' But one thing I must say about Mungie Mackay: he was a straight man.

There were a lot of worthies in this village in Mungie's time. In fact, the Lithuanians were comin' across here because they were afraid to go on army service with the Russian Tsar. Well, there were too many o' them comin' across and nobody could actually put their names into English. One of them got the name of Peter Fifty-six. He was known all his days in Newtongrange by that name. Even when he was buried Peter Fifty-six was put on his box. It was because he was the fifty-sixth Pole to come across to work in the Lady Victoria. Some o' them thought that they would manage to get into Bellshill, to the clay mines there and the brickworks, but they came through this way.

Another one was standing in the village at a shop right on the corner, when a traveller asked him, 'Could you tell me where Shaw's shop is in Newtongrange?' And the only answer he got was, 'Me no' ken.' 'What is your name?' the traveller asked. He says, 'Shop window.' Well, the shop window had a big display in it o' Bird's Custard. So the traveller said to him: 'Is your name Bird?' He said, 'No.' 'You Custard?' He said, 'Yes.' So he got the name o' Mick Custard all his days in Newtongrange. And Mick was a lad that was keen to get on; in fact he got intae Newbattle School.

Well, in those days it was the Parish Council. And there was always one name that came up on the Parish Council that never received any opposition: Mungo Mackay. In these days he was the only J.P. in the village. But at no time would Mr Mackay sit in the chair. He always liked to listen. And if there were any miners' names to be put on the short leet, Mungie would turn round and tell them: 'Ye can't put that man on the short leet, because he's one o' ma best miners.'

He used to come down through the village, walking with his stick, to see how everything was lookin'. And down near the bottom pub there wis a man wi' the name o' Toshie Moffat. Toshie couldna be bothered doin' his garden at any time. So Mr Mackay sent for Toshie to come up to the office one day, and he said to him: 'Toshie, yer gairden's a disgrace tae the raw. What are ye gaun tae dae aboot it?' Toshie looked at Mungie and he said: 'Mr Mackay, ye havenae seen ma gairden right because,' he said, 'there are tatties planted in ma gairden.' 'Oh, no, no, Toshie,' he says, 'they're no tatties planted in your gairden.' He said, 'The tatties,' he says, 'that you're talkin' about are all long gress.' 'Well,' Toshie says, 'ye'll hae tae gaun doon tae the auld ferm because,' he says, 'ma tatties are comin' up doon there.'

Mungo Mackay and the Green Table

When Newtongrange Star's football ground was being laid out, Mungie had friends come to visit him. And there was an old soldier, Wullie Philip, who worked on the boiler fires who used to go on a drinkin' spree. Wullie had been across by the football park and who does he see there but Mr Mackay and his friends. So he walks up tae Mungie and he says tae him, 'Ah wonder, Mr Mackay, if ye wid be as guid enough as tae gie me a len o' half-a-croon?' So Mungie Mackay puts his hand in his pocket and says tae him: 'Wullie,' he says, 'there's yer half-croon. Will ah keep it off yer pey?' 'Oh, no, no,' says Wullie, 'what ye gie tae a freend ye cannae draw back.' Ah can tell ye that story because Mungie told me himself.

Well, the day when Mungo Mackay died it was agreed that the contractors of the different pits would be the pall-bearers of his coffin. And the pit finished early that day because there were to be a service held in the Newbattle Parish Church. The church couldn't take in everybody. The bearers took in the coffin and placed it near the pulpit. And they had a hymn, a prayer, a reference made to Mr Mackay's great works. And then another hymn. Then everybody lined up to go into the new cemetery. And when the funeral got to the graveyard gates there were about twice as many people standin' there as what was in the procession comin' up from the kirk.

GEORGE WESTON

My first recollection o' meetin' Mr Mackay was when I had been started only about six or seven months as an apprentice electrician underground. That would be about 1930–31. You wis known as the bell boy. You looked after the bells, that was your job—lookin' after the wires that run across the sides o' the roads and coupled tae the engines. And you had to do that for about two year before you started doin' anything else.

Anyway in ma first year at work, along wi' several other youths frae the village, we were gallavanting round about and we came to Newbattle School. We went into the playground and there was a window half-open. So we opened the window full, and went into the school, three or four of us, and travelled through the school to the gymnasium, caperin', you know. Graffitti's not jist a modern phenomenon, because we were writin' on the wa's, rude words and everything! In the gymnasium we had a bit o' a carry-on! The janitor's house was quite near the gymnasium. Well, he heard the rumpus in the school, he followed the noise round—him on the outside and us on the inside—and when we came out the windae he grabbed us.

So he took all our names. There were no police concerned. And the next day ma father, who also worked in the pit, got a line on his token that he was to take me up to see Mr Mackay. Ye had tae have a collar and tie on. You actually never saw Mr Mackay in the colliery's time, never. Even the officials had to come back to the colliery at night. We went up before the Green Table—and the palaver: he ignored ye until ye wis jist a bag o' nerves and then he spoke. And the policeman was there, Frank Taylor, standin' beside him. I don't know if he was attached to the local constabulary or no', but he was regularly at the colliery. I was really worried to death. Mr Mackay spoke about how my grandfather would be ashamed. My grandfather—that's on my mother's side— was an elder o' the church. Mr Mackay talked about the shame that ah wis bringin', and if ah carried on like that ah'd land in borstal. Then he passed the sentence. Now I was the only apprentice, the rest that had gone intae the school worked underground. He fined the other two 2/6d. each. And because ah wis the youngest his sentence on me wis that I was to attend the night school for two years!

I'll tell you one thing, it did me a very much greater good than what it would ha' done if ah had been sentenced to two years in Borstal. Because the further education that ah had at night school gave me the sort o' method to go forward again and keep studyin'. So it seems that there's a lot in education instead o' punishment, because we had actually committed a crime, a crime that possibly we'd be sent down for now.

That was ma first occasion I met Mr Mackay. But I don't think he should be romanticised because he was actually a tyrant.

The next personal experience I had wi' Mr Mackay wis in 1938. When the Munich Crisis was on I had an urge tae join the Air Force. Ah wis an electrician in a section underground at the time. And Rutherford, the chief electrician, wouldn't let me away. Ah needed a reference for the Air Force and he wouldn't write a reference. I wasn't allowed to get away—I was needed at the pit. So I went and asked if I could see Mr Mackay. So ah went in and ah saw him and ah told him I wanted to join the Forces and Mr Rutherford wouldn't give me ma reference. So he says, 'Jist you go away back to your work,' he says, 'and I'll see about it.' The next morning on ma token there was an envelope and in the envelope was a nice written reference. So he had become involved so that I could get to the Air Force. That wis the last time I ever saw Mr Mackay. He died the followin' year. I was in the Air Force at the time he died.

But I was invalided out the Air Force in 1941 and by that time I wanted tae further ma education. Ah went in for minin' and ah got a diploma in minin' at Heriot Watt College. I finished up ma time in the pits years later as an official.

I was born in Newtongrange and I've lived in Newtongrange all my life, with the exception o' the time I was in the Services durin' the War.

Ah wis an electrician at the time that the contractin' system was on in the Lady Victoria and ah thought it wis a vicious system. Ye had several men in the pit gettin' big wages at the expense o' the others. One o' the contractors, Wullie Allan, never swore. He didn't sweir. He called men blacks. Ah can remember one day bein' in there at the roadhead next tae the conveyor. It wis a chain conveyor that run down the face and carried the coal intae a cross-loadin' machine which filled it intae the tubs. The coal was comin' on this chain conveyor and pourin' out jist like comin' over a waterfall. And Wullie's sittin' in the end, wi' his feet up on the conveyor, and he says: 'There's some bleck no' fillin' up there!' And the coal was comin' down in a flood! Wi' the profits he made out o' the contractin' system Wullie Allan started a garage business.

Another time I had a breakdown on a switch on a cross-loader and the contractor was over ma shoulder: 'Are ye gaun tae be long? Are ye gaun tae be long? Will ah send the men home?' 'Cause if the men wis sent home he didn't need tae pay them. Ah says, 'Ah'll no' be a minute.' He says, 'Can ye no' cut the switch oot? Bridge it across?' He says, 'Wullie

MacIntosh sometimes daes that.' Ah says, 'Ah'm no' daein' that,' ah says, 'ah'm doin' the job right.' Eventually we got it away. But these were the things that went on. At that time ye wis afraid tae go up and even report a half-an-hour loss o' time. The chief electrician tore ee tae ribbons if ye lost time.

In the Lothian Coal Company the contractors employed their own men, management didn't interfere—at least made as little interference as possible wi' the men they employed. The contractors paid their men a wage, but the contractors bein' on a contract they got the bulk o' the money. Ah had an uncle a contractor, and ma aunt—oh, she was an awfy woman—used tae be annoyed if she hadn't £30 to put in the bank each week. And this was away back in the 1920s, ye know, when ah wis a boy. She wis annoyed if she hadnae £30—and the men were goin' home wi' barely £3. Well, when ah started in the pit as an electrician ah wasn't involved in the contractin' system, but as an observer ah could see what was goin' on. It was a bad, bad system, which when the National Coal Board took over after nationalisation, stopped.

As ah say, Mungo Mackay was actually a tyrant. He could do some pretty vicious things. And some of the things, it's only hearsay, ye know, bein' told by my parents—so the truth o' it I can't say. But one or two things I did know the truth o' them. Two or three doors from where we stayed there was a family, Miller they called them. Mrs Miller was a widow woman. Her man had worked in the pit, he had died, she had a large family and the only person in the family who was workin' was her oldest son. He worked in the workshops. He got the chance o' a better job out the pits altogether. Then he went and put his notice in, and Mr Mackay sent for him and told him that his mother would lose her house if he left the pit. The son said: 'Ah've got that job—more money and better prospects,' he says, 'ah'm takin' it.' And the pit policeman—the same policeman that ah met at the Green Table, Frank Taylor—served an eviction notice on Mrs Miller. She was evicted from her house with her large family. She went tae stay wi' relations in Gorebridge. The family still stays in Gorebridge but Mrs Miller's dead. I never forget these things.

The next episode—and this was another hearsay story from my parents—was when my father was a young man about eighteen. That would be 1910, 1908, or somethin' like that. He wis what they called a drawer, that's pushin' the hutches after they were loaded. The hutches or tubs used to be ten hundredweight and the Lothian Coal Company altered them to twenty hundredweight—one ton. And the young fellows who were the drawers wanted more money for the larger hutches. And they were refused. So ma father led what they called a steg—a stoppage. And he was called before Mr Mackay. But the drawers refused to shove the hutches unless they received more money. They did eventually get two or three shillins extra on their week's wages. But twenty years later, my uncle—Henry was his name and George was my father's name—my uncle was in for a haulage contract. And he had to go up to Mr Mackay to see about this contract. And Mr Mackay says: 'Is your brother George still misbehavin'?' He had minded o' the steg twenty years before! Eventually Uncle Henry got the contract.

Another time my father received an accident in the pit. And he was lyin' in bed and the policeman—the colliery police-man, Frank Taylor—came to the door and came in to see my father. And he told my father that Mr Mackay suspected that he had received this injury playin' football! He said that he had went to his work wi' the football injury and claimed that he had received the injury in the pit. My father had quite a struggle to get workmen's compensation at that time. That was another thing.

I'll tell you this much, the staff was actually more terrified of Mr Mackay than were the workmen. The staff was absolutely terrified. If they got a summons to go up the stair they went intae a state o' shock!

It used tae be that smokin' was forbidden underground. But they weren't as strict on it in thae times as they are now actually. If anybody was caught smokin' in the pit it was a fine, and the fine was sent tae the Edinburgh Royal Infirmary as a donation—a day's wages.

Now talkin' about the social side o' the colliery and interferin' wi' private life. My father wis very friendly wi' a chap called Davie Pryde. They were brought up together, they played football together and they used tae drink together in the Dean Tavern. Then Davie Pryde became an overman in the pit. Now when a man was put up tae be an official in the Lothian Coal Company—that's an overman—he wasn't allowed to socialise wi' miners. But Davie Pryde still went with ma father and they used tae go drinkin' together. Well, Mungo Mackay sent for Davie Pryde and told him that he had to stop doin' this, and stop drinkin' in the Dean. After that, they still went out together but they had to travel away from the village to drink. They used tae go tae the Justinlees at Eskbank and did their drinkin' there, so that they would-nae co-habit in the Dean. And they used tae gaun as far away as the Juniperlea beyond Pathhead. Once they became on a different level, they weren't allowed to drink together, though they had been friends since school.

There were a lot o' small instances like that, but certainly everybody had a pride in their village. Oo had a lovely park, a lovely bowling green. That policeman we were talkin' about, Frank Taylor, was a member o' the bowling club when ah wis jist a laddie. And when ye went up before Mackay and Frank Taylor's standin' aside Mungo Mackay wi' his uniform on, ye sort o' chuckled tae yourself because on the Saturday night he'd been singin' *Old King Cole was a Merry Old Soul* in the bowlin' club.

As ah say, they were hard times and sort o' happy. But ah wouldnae like tae gaun back tae thae sort o' times in the village. Mungo Mackay wisnae a bad man, he wisnae a good man either. He was a good man for his employer. He was a bad man for his workers. That must be ma opinion. But ah wouldnae say he wis a bad man, no' really a bad man, at heart.

In these days ye could get your job wi' bein' a member o' the bowlin' group, or get a house bein' a member o' the bowlin' club, because Frank Taylor was one o' the leadin' lights in the bowlin' club. Or a Mason—things like that. There wis a lot o' these sort o' things. I'll tell ye all Mungo Mackay's best friends were Masons. There were no doubt about it. All his best friends joined the Masons, all his best friends.

All his foremen were Ayrshire men. Every one o' the foremen: Torrance, the boilermaker, George Humphrey, the head engineer, Duncan, the blacksmith, they were all Ayrshire men. I wouldn't say that you had to be an Ayrshire man before you got a foreman's job. Why it happened, I don't know—whether it was because Mungo Mackay was an Ayrshireman—but all the foremen were Ayrshiremen as well. They were all pretty good at their work.

Now Mungo Mackay's family, well, George Mackay was a disappointment tae his father. He was a softer man, George Mackay. He was one o' the lads—a different chap tae his father, and that's why he was a disappointment. He never went very high in the minin' industry. The wrong son went intae the farmin'.

Well, as ah told ye ah wis in the Air Force at the time Mungo Mackay died. But ah can remember o' bein' told there were a big crowd there. And the story got about that the big crowd was there tae make sure that he wis buried!

BILL STEELE

In 1928 I started work at Whitehill Colliery in Rosewell as an office boy. My wage to start with was eight shillings a week—forty pence. And for that ah started work about half past seven in the morning and finished about six o'clock at night. You worked five-and-a-half days a week. You finished at one o'clock on a Saturday. I didn't live in Rosewell, I lived then where I live today, in Eskbank, between Eskbank Toll and Bonnyrigg. In these days nobody owned cars. Ye had to walk. Buses were quite few.

A year or two later I became a wages clerk and had first-hand experience of the wages being paid to the miners and to surface workers, and also to the brickwork workers. The labourers' wages in these days was thirty shillings a week, or £1.50. The average wage was between £2 and £3 a week, living wage. The cost of living was comparably low, too. At that time, too, a person who earned £5 a week and over didn't need to pay insurance. That was a very big wage in these days, £5 and over.

At Whitehill Colliery, Rosewell—which belonged to the Lothian Coal Company—the average wage in about the 1930s was eight shillings a shift. Tradesmen—skilled men: engineers, fitters, electricians and so on—earned about 8/6d. a day; labourers, as I said, between thirty and thirty-six shillings a week.

When I started work there from 1928 and until about 1930 James Hamilton was the agent at Whitehill Colliery under

James A. Hood. Hood was a millionaire who lived at Midfield House in Lasswade.

In these days, Mr Hamilton reigned supreme at the colliery. He stayed at Rosedale House, Rosewell, just above the colliery. He was quite a character. He had a great interest in the brickworks which was just beside the pit. They used to get the best washer-redd from the colliery at a nominal price, I think it was 1/11d. a ton, so that the best clay went into the bricks. One day he was going along on his usual inspection. There was a man putting bricks from the kiln into a pile. He was only using one hand to do his work. So Mr Hamilton said to him: 'What's wrong? Why are you not using two hands?' The man said to him: 'Oh, one hand at a time is good fishing.' Mr Hamilton said, 'In that case, go to the office and get your line.' The man was sacked. And that's the kind of life it was in these days. You didn't have a shop steward, the unions didn't really have the power that they have today. The boss could sack a man—a moment's notice—and that was it.

As I said, the miner got eight shillings a shift, and a surface labourer six shillings a shift. The lowest rent was about three shillings a week. The best house at Saughree in Rosewell was ten shillings for rent, two shillings for rates, and sixpence— old pennies—for water: 12/6d. a week. It was a very good house and they're still standing today.

In 1928 there were no pithead baths at Rosewell. They were built two or three years afterwards, and the men then found it quite a lot better and cleaner and so did their wives.

Ah remember, too, that at the Co-op in Rosewell at that time the dividend paid was four shillings in the pound. It was a very good dividend indeed, twenty per cent. And it was the officials of the Lothian Coal Company who were the treasurer and secretary of the Co-op.

Well, Mungo Mackay was in charge of three collieries belonging to the Lothian Coal Company in these days:

Easthouses, Lingerwood, and Lady Victoria. After Mr Hamilton died about 1930, Mungo Mackay's son George was in charge of the Whitehill and Polton collieries. But occasionally Mungo Mackay was down at Whitehill and I remember that he came over this day to go down the pit. He was rather a tall man, over six feet. He was in his sixties and he was suffering from heart trouble. He also had a walking stick, going down the pit, and as far as I know he carried it always with him. I think he probably used it to keep his balance when he was down the pit, in case he stumbled. As well as being a clerk I also did first-aid work. And this day he hit his head on one of the surface girders down in the pit. So I had the job when he came up of bandaging the cut on his head. I remember I was impressed by his obvious dominant personality. He would be approximately seventy years of age at that time and he was obviously an ill man, because his complexion was almost purple and his lips were extremely blue. So I wasn't surprised to hear about two years afterwards that he had died.

George Mackay was a different personality, I would say, from his father: more approachable. He lived in Rosedale House in Rosewell, after Mr Hamilton's death. But George didn't follow his father as a great engineer. He confined himself more, I think, to bein' manager down the pit.

I went over to work at Newtongrange later on. Older people, ah think, have respect for Mungo Mackay because the three collieries—Easthouses, Lingerwood and Lady Victoria—always worked at a profit under him prior to nationalisation. Whitehill Colliery and Polton Colliery also worked at a profit until Polton Colliery was flooded. I think Mungo Mackay is remembered as a great engineer more than anything else.[38]

Both at the Rosewell Collieries and the Newtongrange Collieries they had the contracting system, whereby it was the contractor took a gamble driving for the manager, whether it was a hard rock or soft coal he was driving through. If it was hard rock he might not get as much money as he expected. If it was soft coal he might get very well paid for the job. But the contracting system was very popular up to nationalisation. It stopped at nationalisation.

PAT FLYNN

Ah wis born in 1930 in this wee village Rosewell, about three or four miles from Newtongrange, and ah remember hearin' about this God-like figure that went round, this Mungie Mackay.

The power that these chaps had is phenomenal. In Rosewell the pit wis owned by the Lothian Coal Company. The Tavern, where you had your pint o' beer, wis owned by the Lothian Coal Company. The Co-operative Store, where everything was bought—paraffin, saws, salt, vinegar, pepper, food, butcher meat, clothin' (when you could afford it)—it belonged to the Lothian Coal Company. The chemist's belonged to the Company store. And a very important thing at this particular time, relative tae a miner, wis a blacksmith's shop. If ye were a miner ye used tools and these tools ye had tae buy yerself. And if ye get a pick or a knife, they have tae be sharpened. Well, this is where the blacksmith came in. And ah forgot the main thing, the biggest thing o' the bloody lot the Lothian Coal Company owned, wis the houses. They owned the houses.

The Lothian Coal Company they owned ye really, body and soul. Now I can understand the complete power and the dominance this Company had ower the people that lived in Rosewell. Almost every penny that wis made went back tae the Lothian Coal Company. So imagine if you happened tae fall foul o' any o' these Christian chaps like Mungie Mackay! He wis a great Christian chap (and if ye believe that ye believe anything). He wis an absolute tyrant, as far as ah'm led tae believe.

Ah started in Rosewell pit in 1945 and Mungie Mackay died in 1939, so obviously I never met him. But stories aboot Mungo Mackay are legion. There's some fascinatin' stories o' the authority this chap wielded in Rosewell. So ah often thought as ah got older, 'Ah wonder what the hell's fire authority he exerted in Newtongrange?', where he walked up and down the street, where in Rosewell we jist, as far as ah know, appeared in front o' him on odd occasions.

Newtongrange wis where his strong point wis, and accordin' to what ah've heard he completely ruled and dominated the village. Now wi' bein' managin' director o' the Lothian Coal Company his presence sort o' drifted oot tae the surroundin' villages. These surroundin' villages wis Bonnyrigg, Poltonhall, Easthouses, Gorebridge, Dalkeith, Birkenside, and a' these wee places round aboot. And it drifted intae Rosewell tae. His type o' dominance filtered through tae Rosewell to whoever wis in charge o' the pit in Rosewell, the Whitehill colliery.

And I'll gie ye one instance: the fear, the fear that we had. This is a story ah heard when ah started at Whitehill Colliery aboot 1945. I wis led tae believe that it wis true and I've no reason tae doubt it. There wis a big house just up by the pit, Rosedale House, about 300 or 400 yards up the road. Mr Hamilton was the manager o' Rosewell or Whitehill colliery and he lived in Rosedale House. And in the colliery workshops—the blacksmith's shop, the engineerin' shop, the electric shop—if Mr Hamilton happened to be comin' they used tae hae a signal which went, SSSSSSS SSSSSSS—which meant: 'Get workin'!' or 'Get oot the road!' So this went on for years. Every time they heard this SSSSSSS SSSSSSS they used tae scatter, ye know, if they were talking' about a game o' football, or dogs, or pigeons, or whatever, they used tae scatter. This chap Mr Hamilton died. I think it must ha' been aboot 1935 or 1936. And on the day he was gettin' buried the hearse was passin' by the workshops, so the men were peerin' out, lookin', lookin' at this great man passin' in his coffin: 'Oh, look at him, oh!' And all o' a sudden somebody came to the workshops door and went: SSSSSSS SSSSSSS. And they all scattered! Here's Mr Hamilton goin' by in his coffin—and they were still terrified o' him![39]

When ah wis fourteen ah left school and ah got a job as a vanboy in the Rosewell Co-operative Store. It still belonged tae the Lothian Coal Company. Ah wis there about six or nine months, then I decided ah wis gaun tae get another job. So ah telt the manager o' the Co-op—his name wis Mr Kay—that ah wis leavin'. And he says: 'Oh, ye can't leave here.' 'Oh,' ah says, 'but yes ah can.' And he says tae me: 'Well, if ye're leavin' ye have tae get somebody tae put in yer place.' And ah thought this was rather unfair. How should ah run around the villages or the towns tae get somebody tae replace me? That wisnae ma job. But he insisted it wis. So ah insisted ah wouldnae. So ah wis goin' tae leave, and his partin' words tae me wis: 'Well, ah've made sure ye won't get a job up there'—'up there' bein' the Whitehill Colliery.

Now to let ye understand, there wis the colliery, plus a' the workshops—the electric shop, the engineering shop, the blacksmith's shop, the joiner's shop, and the plumber's shop. There were also a brickwork there. And there wis other employments connected wi' the pit. And at this time we were livin' in a Lothian Coal Company house, and ah says tae masel: 'Ah hope ma mother and faither disnae get put oot the hoose because o' this.' But in 1944, as it wis then, we were gettin' tae hae some civilisation intae the place, and nothin' happened. So ah left the Co-op tae go tae a farm, and ah worked there for a few months. But then ah got a job in the Whitehill pit as an apprentice boilermaker. That wis in 1945.

One story ah heard is again aboot the complete dominance o' the Lothian Coal Company ower its employees at Rosewell. This miner had a son and he was leavin' the school at the July. That wis the main time for leavin' school in this area. And the manager o' that colliery bein' Mr Hamilton, sent for him and says tae him: 'Ah believe ye've got a son leavin' school in July?' And the miner promptly replied, 'Yes, sir.' 'Well,' says Mr Hamilton, 'ah've got a job up here at the colliery for him.' And the miner replied, 'Well, ah'm gaun tae try tae get him a job as a tradesman.' Because, tae let ye know, a collier's job, or work in the pit—ye could be oot a job in a jiffy. Whereas if ye were a tradesman ye were practically guaranteed a job, ye were sort o' an elite. So this was what this miner was tryin' tae dae. He wis tryin' tae get his son into a job wi' some sort o' future in it. And he said, 'No, I wid rather ma son tae be a tradesman.' And Hamilton duly replied: 'No, ye jist better bring him up here. Ah've got a job for him in the pit.' The miner pursued the matter, sayin': 'No, ah would rather he got a job as a tradesman.' So it jist came to the point where Mr Hamilton says tae the chap: 'Bring him up here on Monday mornin' or bring the keys o' the house up.' Now this is the dominance of the Lothian Coal Company system. Ah've nae doubt it prevailed in other parts o' the country jist the same—in Fife and Ayrshire.

But what oo're led tae believe is that the power o' Mungie Mackay had itself felt right a' the way through Rosewell. Ye couldnae cough, ye couldnae be sick, ye couldnae be anythin', withoot Mr Mackay or his understudies hearin' aboot it.

There are other stories aboot the complete power they had in Rosewell. If ye had a fruiterer, ye know, a chap goin' round sellin' apples, oranges, potatoes, leeks or whatever, they used tae go frae village tae village. And they started comin' tae Rosewell from the local places, Bonnyrigg or Dalkeith, or somewhere like that. And this interfered wi' the trade o' the

Rosewell Store, which belonged tae the Lothian Coal Company. So the Lothian Coal Company promptly put up posts in the side streets leadin' off the main road, tae stop the outside traders gettin' in, tae make sure that all the trade went back tae the Store, back into the coffers o' the coalowners. Traders could go the main road but the side roads belonged to the Lothian Coal Company. And ah remember thae posts in some bits o' Rosewell, at the top o' Preston Street and Louisa Square. Ah think they're still there.

And to exert their full power the Lothian Coal Company in Rosewell had a polisman. He was called the pit policeman. His name was Mr Goodall. Ah dunno how far back this is, it must ha' been roond aboot 1938, '39. Now he went round the village and he carried out the policy o' Mungo Mackay and enforced Mr Hamilton's rules. And he could come to the hoose and say: 'Out!' Or 'You're fined.' Or 'Come up to the pit.' He was absolutely all-powerful. Ye used tae be terrified o' Mr Goodall. If ye seen him aboot two or three hundred yairds in front ye detoured and got oot o' his road. Terrified!

We had an ambulance at Rosewell which belonged to the Lothian Coal Company. It was a ramshackle thing. A lot o' people ca'ed it a few different names than an ambulance at that time—a cairt, some o' them used tae call it. In the pits in these times deaths and injuries wis very, very frequent. Safety in the mines was non-existent, there wis no such things as safety regulations. And this ambulance used tae rattle frae Rosewell tae the Edinburgh Royal Infirmary regular.

Ah remember goin' in the ambulance once, along wi' ma brither. Ah dunno what age ah wis then. Ah suppose ah'd be aboot six or seven, and we took the scarlet fever. And ah remember o' gettin' wrapped up in these red blankets, a' the tension, people cryin', ye're gaun away, and away tae Loanhead Hospital. Now scarlet fever is very infectious. Oo had rickets and malnutrition and every other bloody disease that wis gaun. Oo had it because oo couldnae feed. Oo werenae gettin' enough money tae feed. Well, ah remember them sayin' ah wis gaun tae hospital and ah wis fair delighted, 'cause ah knew ah'd get something tae eat.

In those times, as ah say, there wis a lot o' accidents in the pits. And I remember once, ma father got injured and he was off an awfy long time. Ma father worked under the contractin' system. The contractin' system was whereby the owners o' the colliery, or their representatives, made a contract wi' one man, and he in turn employed other men. But it wis slave labour, because this man could hire and fire men at a whim. Ma father worked tae a contractor called Anthony Hanley. Ah remember where he lived, in Duke Street, in the middle o' Rosewell. And ah used tae have tae go for ma father's pay occasionally. He had a lot o' accidents but this one particular time he was off an awfy long time. There wis no social security at this time, there wis no money comin' in frae anywhere. The only place you could get money was borrow from yer neebours, or, if you got it frae the Parish, I think there wis a means test that very few people went tae. But ye were allowed tae stay in the Lothian Coal Company house providin' ye'd go back tae the colliery again. So when ye went back tae work again ye started payin' rent and a half.

Now ah remember goin' for ma dad's pay and, whatever it wis—a couple o' pound or whatever—Mr Hanley, the contractor, sittin' behind this table wi' a' the money in front o' him, sayin': 'Tell yer father it's rent and a half this week.' And ah remember him sayin' that for what sounded like bloody years tae me: 'Tell yer father it's rent and a half this week.' I used tae wonder if ma dad had peyed this house ower and ower again.

Ma father used tae work nightshift. He used tae go at nine o'clock at night tae the pit, and his hours wis from then till six in the mornin'. But if he didnae finish his job he'd tae carry on till nine that day or twelve that day—no overtime, no overtime. They were the conditions. And he was workin' in very, very wet conditions. They were probably up tae here in water—instead o' a drip, he'd be up tae here in water. And he'd probably get ninepence for that.

Ah remember ma father comin' home from work—he worked in Rosewell colliery a long, long time—and he come home really tired, dog tired. And ah remember ma mother speakin' tae him: 'What were ye daein'?' An' he says: 'Aw, ah wis puttin' up a girder.' Now at that time ah didnae know what a girder wis. But it's a support underground, an arch-shaped girder, and what ye done wis ye blew a certain amount o' rock down and erected one o' these. Well, nowadays in the pit ye can get anything frae three, four or five people to put one girder up. In those days it wis jist one man put it up hisself.

My father had two very, very serious accidents. He got his ankle broken in two bits and tae the day he died—he died at the age o' 86—the bottom o' his leg looked like a crooked walkin' stick. He was off work wi' that brek ah think round about nine months.

It wis a very hard job establishin' a trade union in Rosewell. Mungie Mackay and the Lothian Coal Company would have nothin' at a' tae dae wi' it. The contractin' system didnae lend itself tae trade unionism. You're frightened tae join a union. Ma dad would be frightened tae join a union. They wouldnae get no permission tae meet anywhere. In fact, they were hassled, as far as ah know. Anybody that tried tae stand oot for the trade union had tae be a very talented guy wi' a lot o' courage tae stand up, because he wid be hounded. If anybody tried tae start a union they'd probably be evicted. There were still stalwarts prepared tae fight against this oppression. Ah remember an old union man, Bobby Neil frae Rosewell. He told me that in thae days, 1925–26 up to 1930 or so, the only wey they could have a union wis tae go round the village. And they went roond the village askin' people wid they join the union? If they decided tae join then they took it in turns every week to go roond the village to collect their two or three pennies. But if management knew this was gaun on they'd send for them and say: 'There won't be a job for you here and there won't be a house for you here.'[40]

Rosewell is a very out of the way place, as a lot o' the minin' villages were. They were very isolated. And we lived in the most deprived poverty ye could get. The housin' conditions was almost the same as Newtongrange—terraced houses, all at the back o' one another. There wis one tap in the house, there were no electricity. There were gas lightin'. There were outside toilets—probably aboot forty yards frae the hooses—and the stuff was collected once a week or so. You can imagine an outside toilet—no flushin' away. It wis terrible, absolutely terrible.[41]

Rosewell was called Little Ireland because there were that many Irish Catholics in it. Now it wisnae called that for nothin'. Ma dad wis born in Ireland and he came across to Scotland. Ah dunno when, it must ha' been in the early '20s or maybe before that. And, funny, but there seemed to be a hell of a lot of Irish people in Rosewell. Ah often wonder as times goes on why were so many Irish people congregated in the one place. And ah wonder was there so many Protestants congregated in the other half o' the Lothian Coal Company set-up, namely, Newtongrange? And ah often wonder tae maself, wis this a policy o' Mungie Mackay or o' the Lothian Coal Company? Ah never heard any concrete evidence to this fashion, but it's always at the back o' ma head. Ah wonder, wis he tryin' to divide and conquer, because we all know the system o' capitalism is divide and conquer. If you go up tae

Rosewell yet and meet some o' the older chaps they still call it Little Ireland. They were predominantly Catholic in Rosewell. And to this day they've got one of the most beautiful churches that's been built in this area.[42]

There were no baths in Rosewell pit whatsoever until the miners got together and decided through a welfare system that the Lothian Coal Company would build the baths. The Company built it and the mineworkers paid. Well, ah remember payin' the 1/6d. a week for the use o' the baths in 1945. Thirty-three shillins a week—that wis ma wages when ah first started in 1945 at the pit as an apprentice boilermaker.

The coalowners were great at startin' up bands and buyin' ambulances and doin' this and that. But it always came frae the wages o' the men. They paid for the silver bands, pipe bands, they paid for street lightin' at one time, and as ah said, they paid for the baths. Ye paid for cap lamps, ye paid for carbide, ye paid for your own tools, ye paid for explosives, ye paid for every bloody thing. When ye'd get your wage ye'd a' this tae come off it.

The social occasion at Rosewell wis the Gala Day, a village Gala Day. It was run by the miners. They'd be probably about 99.7 per cent miners in Rosewell, or mining families. Families in that era were always big. Very, very seldom ye seen two kids in a family. It wis always six, seven, eight, nine, ten. And ye can imagine mothers tryin' tae buy a new jersey, a new pair o' trousers, or a new pair o' sandals or rubbers. And ye used tae try and go oot tae the tatties—potato pickin'—tae try and augment. And everybody would muck in. I mind my mother goin' oot tattie pickin'—there were never any other job.

Can you imagine six men—miners—comin' in tae the hoose, six dirty pair o' trousers, six dirty pair o' socks, no underwear—nae underwear in these days. Ye'd maybe have a semmit, certainly long johns, a shirt, and maybe a coat ye used for travellin' in. Now the miners were lyin' up tae here in water, both sides. You can imagine the task the mothers had tae go through in thae days. Nae tumble dryers, nae washin' machines, nae runnin' water, one fire, and the heatin' o' this water wis a real problem. Ah take ma hat off tae the women o' that era. They must have had some terrible times. But that's the only time I remember my mother workin' at the tatties for a few weeks. And that wis the whole thing behind it—gettin' a new jersey or a new pair o' trousers or a new frock for the bairns for the Gala Day. Gala Days were somethin' in these times. One highlight a year, and that wis oor Gala Day.

I heard another story, it wis about ma wife's uncle, a chap called Tommy Tracy. Ah think he started his apprenticeship as a waggon builder at Newtongrange wi' the Lothian Coal Company about 1920, maybe earlier. And the story he told me frae his own lips wis that ye finished work on the Saturday and ye went home about twelve o'clock. And then ye socialised. Well, their socialisin' at that particular time wis the picture hoose in Nitten. They quite often went there. But once again the power o' the Lothian Coal Company and the people that ran it could stretch beyond all barriers. There wis a damaged waggon. The waggon run away in the pit and they needed some people tae repair this. So the wey the Lothian Coal Company done it wis they got somebody frae the pit tae go down tae the village and get waggon-builders. So wi' the pictures bein' on in the picture hoose this man they sent he'd jist tae go tae the pictures and ask for five waggon-builders. And Uncle Tom told me the names o' the five wis shouted oot in the picture hoose, when the film was still goin' on. And bein' young lads, the five didnae want tae go back tae the colliery tae fix this waggon. So they hid in the picture hoose. The projectionist or the manager widnae shut off the film, so the next thing they did wis open the curtains up—then they spied the five young lads. The five o' them were marched up tae the pit tae repair this damaged waggon. It jist shows ye the power o' the Lothian Coal Company and the people that ran it—how it could streitch intae anywhere in the village: picture houses, houses, pubs, anythin'. It makes ye think.

Tommy Kerr

Well, the early 1920s and 1930s was the only time that recollections o' Mackay ever came to me. What I mean is, I stayed in East Lothian at that time and it wis 1949 before ah wis transferred tae work in Lady Victoria colliery at Newtongrange. But most miners before the 1939 War that wanted tae transfer never did, as they felt that the attitude o' Mackay and the Lothian Coal Company wis such that they maintained a pressure on the working class in their area that wisnae very healthy.

Ah started in the pits in East Lothian in 1926. Now miners in the Lothians area used to talk about 'up the braes'—Newtongrange and that area—in whispers. They used to say that, 'If there's one place that ah widna like tae work it's up in the area where this man Mackay has the control and the terror struck in the hearts o' the workmen.' And no doubt when ye met in social activities it was sure to crop up that something had happened in the Lothians area where Mackay had some say.

In fact, word came tae us on many occasions that some o' the contractors had contracts that made the condition that they had to stay in the pit irrespective of what had happened durin' breakdowns or other stoppages. And they had tae stay in the pit till they completed their task. In fact, when ah come intae the Newtongrange area—and it wis under nationalisation by then—some o' the contracts were still on the same basis: they must be cleaned off before they could leave the colliery.

Well, the reliable sources about Mackay wis some o' his old contract friends. Ah don't think ah should mention their names, other than to say that they used tae refer tae Mackay as bein' 'a severe man but a just man.' And ee met the odd person that wis employed on these contracts that had no time for the contractors. They related circumstances that they felt should be well known in regards to Mackay's attitudes tae his workers. For instance, if he was movin' through the village, which he did often, tae see that his 'subjects' kept everythin' in order, he used tae stop the governor's car and point tae a piece o' paper on the road and no matter who it was—'Pick that up, please.' And his attitude o' authority was borderin' on Fascism. He wis a dictator in a community.

The contractors, of course, were the first line o' his defence. He employed a man tae be an overseer or somebody in control of a section o' workmen. And he wid pay him so much per light—they got a set amount for every miner's lamp—or so much per ton that the workmen produced. And these contractors got inflated wages, wages much above the ordinary person, and they acted as spies. Similarly there were other men in the pit that succumbed, because ah suppose a man o' his ilk knew the weaknesses and strengths o' men and he could pick them to convey information to him.

In Newtongrange it wis a common thing for people to inform on other miners. They were known that wis ready tae tittle-tattle and tell stories. In fact, ah believe most o' the contractors were used. There wis one at the Toll—and ah widnae care whae heard me say this, he's dead now—but Allan o' the Toll, he seemed tae be notorious. And he was a man that was never oot o' the church. In fact, they had a church o' their own. I think it wis either the Plymouth Brethren or some o' these organisations, and he was never oot o' the church.

Now this man Allan, accordin' tae workmen that worked

under him, he used tae sit at the back o' the pans, like a boatman keepin' the strokes, and he used tae sit tae give them the shovel rhythm. That's the type o' man he wis. He used tae go through the motions—without a shovel, of course! These things disgusted me when ah knew that human beings did them.

Allan had taken seriously ill and they took him to the Infirmary. And his next man had tae take the lines intae the Infirmary, when they collected the lines and the pays, and Allan made the pays up in the Royal Infirmary.

Ye can appreciate too that in these days the contractors had a big say with Mackay. He used to summons them to special meetings, gettin' his reports in the spy fashion, and weedin' out any chance o' militancy o' any description or opposition from workmen in the community.

Well, I had no actual personal contact with Mungie Mackay. But ah lived in the East Lothian minin' community, was militant in the trade union movement in the Lothians, and was well aware of the activities of Mungie Mackay.[43] Ah was aware o' his power over the workers and his representation of the Lothian Coal Company. There's no doubt, if ever there were a reputation that could make money for the employers, he was the one—at the expense of the employees. The contracts that Mungie Mackay had made still persisted when ah come to represent miners in Midlothian after 1949. Allowances, even agreements, were ignored in many instances; and it was evident from what happened durin' the periods from when Mungo Mackay had died that this continued to carry on.

Many o' the Newtongrange miners, you know, in the wintertime never saw their children in daylight. In fact, many of them went back home after the children were asleep and they never even seen them except if they looked into the bedroom before they went to their work.

In these days ah suppose that the power o' the employing class had a true representation in the shape o' Mungie Mackay. He was, of course, a member o' the local Masonic Lodge. In fact, he was appointed Grand Master and his contacts wi' the elite o' the community of course assisted him in playin' his part. He could get a whole host o' information about the activities o' miners by means o' his association with the local Freemasons' Lodge.

He was a leadin' figure in the Church o' Scotland, closely wi' his Masonry. But he was a fly man. He was never sectarian for one section o' the church. Ah believe that his association wi' Roman Catholicism was pretty well known in the locality. Well, ah believe he was friendly wi' the local priests and other people and he conferred wi' them. Ah don't know what the purpose wis but ah leave it tae your own thoughts to guess what he'd be conferrin' about! There's no doubt that he used the church as a means o' controllin' the miners in the pits. Many people that ah know in Newton-grange and in the locality got promotion as a consequence o' bein' seen in the church by Mackay. Mackay was acceptable to every religion because ah don't believe he discriminated. He didn't discriminate to any degree.

In fact, it's a wonder tae me frae the stories that ah heard that they hadnae an obelisk that he could sit in and gather his subjects, because he was a great man for the church. And he used the fear o' the church on many o' the people that he come in contact wi' that disagreed wi' him.

There wis one man o' the name o' King. It wis before ma time. He had come to the area and he wis disgruntled and dissatisfied and din a bit o' organisation. I believe he come from the Fife area. He put up some resistance tae the exploitation that went on. But he seemed to be the type that didnae do it in the fashion tae collect support frae others. And Mackay, of course, ears always tae the ground, sent for him. Now this was the type o' man he was. When he interviewed them the Company's policeman sat beside him; and if a man went intae his office and didnae take off his cap he got a bollickin'. If he went intae his office withoot a collar and tie he wis sent home tae put a collar and tie on, so that Mackay could speak to him! And he had tae stand tae attention a' the time that he was bein' reprimanded.

Well, this man King, there were whisperins throughout the Lothians at the time. And ah can remember well that Mackay had called him into the office. King had a young family and Mackay told him tae immediately go and get some way tae transport his furniture. And Mackay's thugs put his furniture oot in the street long before he got reasonable time, and he wis ushered out the community.

How Mackay used tae operate, he used tae choose a time that men were employed and he used tae send somebody frae their work tae go and do a job. Well, if they didnae do it they were sacked. So that wis the threat that he had held over their head. And you always got in that type o' community folk that were prepared tae dae the worst possible things against their fellow humans.

Mackay used tae take his horse tae go round the village. And if he seen a man's garden wi' a tremendous amount o' weeds in it he used to call him in, warn him tae get it din and he had two days tae do it, withoot time off his work. And if it wasn't done Mackay would see that it wis done and he would keep it off the man's wages. So Mackay used tae pick a man from the pithead, send him to that man's garden with the tools and keep him employed there, and kept off the man's wages the equivalent o' what he paid the other man.

The powers o' Mackay was so great that even if a man didnae attend his work he could phone the local Dean Tavern and instruct the barman: 'This man's not, if he comes in, he's not to receive any drink. He's not to get a pint.' The Dean

Tavern wis run by a Committee o' the clerical staff and Mungie's boys, tae control it. So much went to the community, likes o' Gala Days and other organisations. And he was fly: he made sure that the organisation was pretty tight in that respect.

Now whenever a man o' Mackay's ability and calibre needed constant attendance o' a policeman, ah think ye'll appreciate that there's something wrong. Because if a man wis supposed tae commit some misdemeanour in the pit Mackay used tae send for him and he used to have to go into the office, take off his cap and wait until he was told tae speak. If they hadnae a collar and tie on on many occasions he sent them home tae get a collar and tie on and come back before he would interview them. And the Company policeman sat beside him for no other reason than to act as a bodyguard.

Mackay, whilst a' these activities wis gaun on, must have had a broad outlook as far as knowin' what the community was doin' wis concerned. Because if any organisation was set up he used to query it and find out what its intentions was, and every step was taken to ensure that he was well informed. Mackay was the type o' man that personally ah'm no' vexed that ah didnae meet!

Ah always remember a fellae in Newtongrange, Stephen Weston, tellin' me there were occasions in the early 1930s when there were laddies of about fifteen and sixteen and they had pocket money, because they were workin' in the pit. He can remember aboot fourteen laddies, ken, runnin' thegither, and they had stopped in front o' the Institute. And they were outside, discussin' what they were goin' to do durin' their holidays. And Mungie had seen thir lads when he was passin' by. And it jist showed ye the kind o' mentality he had, that he was gaun tae snuff anything in the bud that wisnae tae his likin'. So he drew up the old horse and he cried some o' them over tae his side. So he asked them what they were discussin', ye ken. 'Aw, oo're jist discussin' aboot gaun campin'. Oo're gaun tae the Borders and oo're talkin' aboot hirin' tents and the rest o' it.' So the bold Mungie, of course, bein' the wise man that he was, in his own interests he telt them tae pick spokesmen and tae come up and see him. And they did. He gave them things, ye know, an allowance o' money or somethin', and helped them wi' some o' their equipment, and kept in contact so that he could keep his ear tae the ground.

He tolerated the trade union movement but more or less that was all that he did. The union of course wis the Mineworkers' Federation o' Great Britain. The Lothians area had a Board o' their own. In fact, ah believe ah wis the youngest delegate elected tae the Board. There had been twenty-odds at one time but when ah went on ah think it wis either eighteen or nineteen. That wis in the early '30s, aboot six or sieven year before the war. Them in the Lothians didnae care very much for the representatives that were chosen by the Newtongrange folk. For instance, John Rutherford. He was a man that wis the joint branch chairman. At one time, ee ken, it wis three pits in one branch: Lingerwood, Easthouses and Lady Victoria. Well, we broke that doon tae when we came here efter the war, because we formed a joint committee and broke away and elected our own officials. The only thing that ah can ever recollect about relations that existed between Mungo Mackay and the Union wis when Alex Cameron wis appointed secretary for the Lothians. And ah always remember Alex Cameron sayin' it wis like tryin' tae open a safe tae get into the Newtongrange area as a trade union official. Trade union membership wis lower in the Newtongrange area than elsewhere. But the point is this that they were organised in a sense. When ah come up here in 1949 we insisted on a closed shop, of course. Ah jist used tae get thirty names. Ah can remember takin' in thirty names tae Alex Meek, who was manager, and sayin': 'Alex, yer pit's standin', son, unless ye tell thae folk they'll hae tae join the Union.' And it happened. But that wis after Nationalisation, ee ken. We were in a much stronger position tae put pressure on them then.

But in Mungo Mackay's time John Rutherford was a checkweigher appointed by the men and no doubt on many occasions Mackay used the psychology o' imposition. He would ask a trade union official like John Rutherford to go to the office and he would keep him waitin' and waitin' and waitin'. This was one o' his methods o' gettin' the first blow in in any negotiations that might have to take place.

Well, when men were summoned before Mackay, they used to say, before goin': 'Ah'm up before Mackay—the Green Table for me the day.' And Mackay used to tell them that any more misdemeanours they would be dismissed, their families would suffer, and 'I'll be monitorin' your activities frae now on.' And they were told in no uncertain fashion. Many men left his office wi' the threats that he'd create circumstances that wasnae good for the health o' the family. There is no doubt the circumstances then was a continual threat over their head if they had been up before the Green Table.

But Mackay was an able person, in the sense he carried out the directors' requests to control the masses o' workmen that worked in the Lothian Coal Company's pits. The only thing that ah would say in his favour, because when ah came tae Newtongrange and descended the Lady Victoria pit, wi' its long haulage ways in the pit bottom, I immediately asked and enquired whae wis responsible for most o' the development in the haulage roads. They were brick-arched. And they says, oh, it wis Mackay himself. So at least he was a good minin' engineer.

In fact, of course, a lot o' it was slave labour, in the sense that miners werenae paid for their work. If he went doon a roadway he used tae walk—ah believe he was a man of aboot five feet ten—doon the road and tae hold his walkin' stick tae his forehead and the point o' it stickin' in the air. And if that stick touched any of the roof instructions were immediately given tae get it heightened. If it wis somebody's fault they never got paid. They had tae put it up above that height. And if he had not carried out that policy in the early years in developin' Lady Victoria it wid ha' been closed many years earlier than 1981. The roadways were a credit tae ony miner or minin' engineer.

But many o' the nice things that ye could say about a person like that were destroyed when some o' the local women might have an argument about children on the dryin' green. And he used tae send for the husbands to the office and instruct them that he didn't want community upheavals, that they must have a word with their wives, they must not quarrel over children, etc., etc.

Mackay of course as a man didnae associate very much wi' the community. But ah can remember havin' conversation wi' his son George. After nationalisation in 1947 ah met George on many occasions. He was in the managerial class. He did relate on twae or three occasions that he couldna have lived wi' his father because o' the type o' man he was. In fact, Mungo Mackay used to get his own family regimented. They'd get oot their bed in the mornin' and the drill had to be carried out: they had to wash, spruce theirsel up, line up, and be inspected before they could sit down at the breakfast table! So it showed you the kind o' attitude that the man had in life. He seemed to have been a very dominant personality, wi' the old ideas o' keepin' folk under subjection to his will.

NOTES

1 The strike was almost certainly the national miners' minimum wage strike of 1 March to mid-April 1912. The minutes, preserved in the National Library of Scotland, acc. 4312, of the Mid and East Lothian Miners' Association contain no reference to any other strike at Newtongrange or Newbattle in that year.

2 The Dardanelles or Gallipoli campaign began in February-March 1915 with an unsuccessful attempt by Allied warships to force their way through the Straits in order to relieve Turkish pressure on the Russian Tsar's army in the Caucasus. British and Allied troops were landed in April at Gallipoli but were finally evacuated in January 1916. British casualties in the campaign totalled 214,000. J.E. Edmonds, *A Short History of World War I* (Oxford, 1951), 107–119.

3 James A. Hood (1859–1941) was a younger son of the coalmaster Archibald Hood who had begun work as an engineman but had acquired pits in Ayrshire and leased Whitehill colliery at Rosewell, Midlothian, from 1856 before moving to develop his coal interests in South Wales. Archibald Hood founded the Lothian Coal Company in 1890, when Whitehill colliery was amalgamated with the Newbattle collieries of the Marquis of Lothian, who became chairman of the new Company until 1900. James A. Hood was general manager of the Company from 1890 until 1902, when he succeeded his father as managing director, and from 1911 until 1941 was chairman of the Company, a position his father had held from 1900 until his death in 1902. It was Archibald Hood who brought Mungo Mackay (1867–1939), born at Auchinleck in Ayrshire, the son of

a draper, from Hood's father-in-law's colliery at Ballochmyle in that county in 1894 to manage the Lothian Coal Company's Polton colliery in Midlothian. Mackay became closely associated with James A. Hood and was appointed manager at Newtongrange in 1895. James A. Hood was a Midlothian County Councillor from 1889 and was closely involved with many of his father's projects, including the Rosewell Co-operative Store founded in 1862 and the public house or tavern opened in that village in 1909, and the 'Gothenburg' Dean Tavern, founded in 1899 at Newtongrange. He approved the Newtongrange Picture Palace or cinema built by the Lothian Coal Company in 1913 and assisted Newtongrange Star Football Club in building its new sports ground and 900-seat grandstand in 1924. With Mungo Mackay James A. Hood played a leading part in the building of company housing for miners of the Lothian Coal Company at Newtongrange, Easthouses and Rosewell. In 1924 he founded the Hood Chair of Mining at Edinburgh University, in conjunction with Heriot Watt College, and was made an honorary LL.D. by the University in 1928. At his death in 1941 Hood's total estate amounted to £436,000 and included investments in 103 different companies, but most of his wealth was invested in the Lothian Coal Company. His obituary by Dr Michael Cotterill—whose researches into the Lothian Coal Company and all aspects of mining in Midlothian place everyone who consults them greatly in his debt—is in *Dictionary of Scottish Business Biography* (Aberdeen, 1986), Vol.I, 42–45.

4 The Coal Mines Act, 1911, made fourteen the minimum age for employment underground.

5 The Mines Eight Hours Act of 1908 established the maximum hours of labour as eight per day, plus winding time—i.e., the time (which varied from pit to pit according to depth and extent of underground workings) taken by miners to go from the pithead to their working place underground and back up again at the end of their shift. See R. Page Arnot, *The Miners* (London, 1949), Vol.I, 335–6.

6 The history of the Dean Tavern, a Gothenburg public house opened in 1899 by the Lothian Coal Company and of which Mungo Mackay was a committee member from 1899 until 1917 and chairman from 1917 until 1939, has been set thoroughly in the context of the development of Newtongrange and the Lothian Coal Company, by Alasdair Anderson in his excellent *The Dean Tavern: a Gothenburg Experiment* (Newtongrange, 1986).

7 *The Dalkeith Advertiser*, 14 April 1921, reported that: 'Irritated, apparently, at the continuance of pumping operations at the various local collieries and at the arrival of reinforcements of pumpers and firemen to carry on the work, the strikers resolved that this state of matters could not be allowed to continue. Following upon a meeting held at the Dalkeith Burns Fountain, a procession of about a thousand miners marched to Newtongrange and demanded the withdrawal of the 'safety' hands. Mr Mungo Mackay, the colliery agent, intimated to Mr Peter Chambers, the miners' agent, that it rested with the employees of these particular pits to determine whether or not pumping work was to proceed in the mutual interest of the company and the pit workers themselves, as a stoppage of the pumps would mean further delay before the miners could eventually resume their coal getting duties. A meeting of the Newbattle miners was arranged, and it practically unanimously called for the withdrawal of the men at the engines and pumps, only two men voting in favour of the work being continued. The step was accordingly taken of abandoning the work at the pumps at Newbattle.' Peter Chambers and a checkweighman were later convicted at Edinburgh Sheriff Court of forming part of a riotous mob 'which interfered with Mungo Mackay, agent, Newbattle Colliery, William Carson, manager of the Lady Victoria pit, and others who were on duty there engaged in maintaining the boiler fires . . . and by intimidation and threats of violence compelled them to draw the boiler fires and to cease from pumping operations, whereby risk of serious damage was incurred'; and of a similar offence the same day at Arniston

Collieries. They were sentenced to two months' imprisonment each. A Smeaton miner who was charged only with the first offence was sentenced to one month's imprisonment. *Dalkeith Advertiser*, 26 May 1921.

8 The Arniston Coal Company had two pits, the Emily and the Gore, at Arniston, about a mile and a half south of Newtongrange.

9 Daniel Stewart's, now merged with Melville College, was founded in 1855 and became one of the Edinburgh Merchant Company's fee-paying schools.

10 The decay, accompanied by the closing of Lady Victoria colliery in 1981, into which Newtongrange had fallen by the early 1980s when Archie Wilson made these comments, was arrested and reversed in vigorous manner by Midlothian District Council and other bodies through a programme of rehabilitation and new building at the village, which has been made a conservation area.

11 Bryans colliery dated from at least the first half of the eighteenth century. See Baron F. Duckham, *A History of the Scottish Coal Industry*. Vol.I, 1700–1815 (Newton Abbot, 1970), 48.

12 The Act of 1842 prohibited the employment underground of women and girls and of boys under the age of ten years.

13 The Derby Scheme was launched in October 1915 by the Earl of Derby as Director of Recruiting and was aimed at reconciling the demands of the army for men with the manpower needs of industry, calling up groups of men as they were wanted, and taking single men first. But the response of the latter was inadequate to preserve the graduated principle, and in January 1916 the Military Service Act replaced voluntary recruitment by conscription. See B.H. Liddell Hart, *History of the First World War* (London, 1970), 269.

14 Lingerwood House, Mungo Mackay's residence opposite the entrance to the Lady Victoria colliery, was demolished in the late 1950s.

15 The immigrants were evidently Lithuanians rather than Poles.

16 Rosslynlee Hospital is near Penicuik; Dobbie's is a well-known nursery and gardening centre near Dalkeith.

17 Sir Charles Carlow Reid (1879–1961) began work as a clerk in the office of the Fife Coal Company in 1893, became general manager in 1939, and was Production Director of the Coal Board in Scotland 1942–43 and in Britain 1943–48.

18 Alasdair Anderson, *op. cit.*, 105, says the Tin Kirk was the Ebenezer Church and that the Church of Christ was known locally as 'Allan's Church'.

19 According to *The Lothian Coal Company Ltd: A Short History* (Leith, 1946), 30, the profit the Company made in 1926–27 was £148,984, which was less than in any of the preceding five years. In 1923–24, the year of the Franco-Belgian occupation of the Ruhr, centre of the German coal industry, profit had been £305,543.

20 In Britain the number of insured unemployed between 1922 and 1930 never fell below one million, and in January 1922 was over two million. B.B. Gilbert, *British Social Policy 1914–1939* (London, 1970), 312–14.

21 James Reid meant two hundred years ago: serfdom was not abolished for miners in Scotland until 1799. Coal had been mined at Newtongrange—originally by the monks of Newbattle Abbey—from the thirteenth century onward.

22 See above, note 7.

23 According to the *Glasgow Herald* of 14 April 1921, a company of the Highland Light Infantry arrived early the previous day to guard collieries at Newbattle and Bonnyrigg, and at Ormiston in East Lothian.

24 The 1921 strike—or lock-out, as it was—lasted thirteen weeks, from 1 April until 1 July.

25 See above, note 19. The profit the Company made in 1921–22 was £193,236.

26 Mrs Jane Paxton of Bonnyrigg recalled in an interview with me in June 1981 that she had come to know Mungo Mackay well after she began work at the age of eighteen in 1916 at the office at Lady Victoria colliery. 'Mr Mackay asked me one day what church ah went to and ah said ah went to Newbattle Church. He said, "Oh, well, ah've been to them all—Cockpen Church,

Lasswade Church, Newbattle Church—and they all preach the same.'"

27 Lord Chelmsford (1868–1933), Viceroy of India 1916–21, First Lord of the Admiralty in the first Labour Government, 1924, was, at the time of the opening of Newtongrange Welfare Park, chairman of the national Miners' Welfare Committee. A full report of the opening of the Park—at which, contrary to James Reid's recollection, Mungo Mackay presided as president of Newtongrange Gala Day Commitee—is in the *Dalkeith Advertiser*, 16 September 1926.

28 Burgari Quinto owned two chip and ice-cream shops in Newtongrange. 'Mr Quinto was the one man in the village who ignored the summons to appear in front of Mungo Mackay's "Green Table". "Tell Mackay to come and see me," he is reported to have said and there was nothing Mr Mackay could do. Mr Quinto owned his own shops and indeed most of the other shops at the top of the village. He was beholden to no one in Newtongrange.' Alasdair Anderson, *op.cit.*, 105.

29 Andrew Clarke (1868–1940), a friend of Keir Hardie, was secretary 1919–40 of the Mid and East Lothian Miners' Association, president of the National Union of Scottish Mine Workers 1932–1940, M.P. for North Midlothian in 1923–24 and 1929, and a manager of Edinburgh Royal Infirmary. See William Knox (ed.), *Scottish Labour Leaders, 1918–1939: a Biographical Dictionary* (Edinburgh, 1984), 77–8. The book referred to by Robert Pearson has not been identified.

30 Smeaton or Dalkeith colliery was owned by A.G. Moore and Co. Ltd.

31 The Moat colliery at Roslin was owned by the Shotts Iron Co. Ltd.

32 The Independent Labour Party nationally was founded in 1893 by Keir Hardie and other parliamentary socialists. The Social Democratic Federation, founded in 1881/84 as a Marxist organisation, was retitled the Social Democratic Party in 1908, and with the adhesion of some other socialist groups became in 1911 the British Socialist Party a majority of whose members amal-

gamated with other socialist groups in 1920 to form the Communist Party of Great Britain.

33 Andrew Anderson (? 1887–1965) worked in the blacksmiths' shop at Newbattle collieries but was victimised because of his trade-union activities. He studied accountancy and became chief cashier of the Scottish Miners' Approved Society. He was elected a Midlothian County Councillor as early as 1910 and remained on the Council for many years.

34 See above, note 6. J.C. Murray was a committee member of the Dean Tavern from 1917 until 1939, and chairman 1939–45. Alasdair Anderson, *op. cit.*, 148–9.

35 The late Tommy Thomson had an encyclopedic knowledge of mining and of Newtongrange but he was not the easiest of persons to interview. He could not be persuaded in this interview to enlarge on his earlier experience of employment with the Lothian Coal Company. J.R. Wilson was presumably manager of Gilmerton pit, though there was a J.R. Wilson who was managing director of the Fordel Mains Co. Ltd, whose colliery at Fordel was two miles south of Dalkeith. A.S. Cunningham, *Mining in Mid and East Lothian* (Edinburgh, 1925), 115.

36 For Arniston Coal Co. Ltd see above, note 8. Niddrie and Benhar Coal Co. Ltd owned Newcraighall, Woolmet and Niddrie pits. Billy Ritchie played for Rangers in the 1960s.

37 Admiral John Jellicoe (1859–1935), Commander-in-Chief of the British Grand Fleet from 1914 and later First Sea Lord, was made an earl in 1925.

38 Polton colliery ceased production when it was flooded in 1933 but it continued as a pumping pit for Whitehill colliery until the latter closed in 1961.

39 James Hamilton, a director of the Lothian Coal Company Ltd and general manager of Whitehill and Polton collieries and brickworks, died at the age of sixty-nine in October 1929, and was buried in Hawthornden cemetery. The chief mourners included Mungo Mackay and James A. Hood. Hamilton was unmarried. *Dalkeith Advertiser*, 31 October and 7 November 1929.

Notes

40 The late Bobby Neil declined to be interviewed by me about his recollections of mining and trade unionism at Rosewell.

41 For some other recollections of life and work at Rosewell and Whitehill colliery in the era of Mungo Mackay, see I. MacDougall, 'Towards an oral history of Rosewell', in *A Sense of Place: Studies in Scottish Local History* (Edinburgh, 1988), 109–121.

42 St Matthew's, Rosewell, is described by Colin McWilliam, *The Buildings of Scotland: Lothian* (Harmondsworth, 1980), 408, as 'A highly original church of yellow stock brick . . . by Archibald Macpherson, finished in 1926.'

43 Tommy Kerr considered that Mungo Mackay always kept close contact with other coal companies in the Lothians. 'It was evident that they worked a system o' blacklistin' if somebody had what they termed a 'notorious' background—a militant person that was prepared to do somethin' to get his rightful deserts.' Mr Kerr said he had worked at some point in the late 1920s for about six months at Smeaton colliery, Dalkeith, but left after a row with the under-manager to whom he said: 'Desist. Ah'm goin' away tae work elsewhere because ah dinnae like yer attitude.' However, he had gone back to work at Smeaton not long afterwards. 'Ah jist worked a couple of days. I didnae leave. I wis despatched out. What happened wis ah wis getting known in the Lothians area as a trade union representative, or somebody that was prepared to organise and fight. And ah can always remember a note bein' left when I came up [the pit], to call at the offices. So ah went up tae the offices and there was one helluva row. J.D. Allan, he says: 'It wis a mistake oo made employin' ee.' He says, 'There werenae nae vacancies. And oo jist noticed yer cards when oo wis gaun through them.' So ah says, 'Come off it. Whae are you tryin' tae kid?' So he wis the same man that wis operatin' after nationalisation and him and I we used to have some goes! I said, 'I can always remember you, Bill. Do you remember when ee sacked a man because his face didnae fit?' He minded a 'right.'

Glossary

bide	stay
birl	spin round
bourgate (or boutgate)	a road by which miners could reach the surface, or a road travelling round a shaft, or a road from one seam to another
brushing	removal of part of the roof or pavement of a coal working in order to heighten the roadway
cage	lift or platform used in the vertical shaft of a colliery to transport men, coal or materials
cannel	bituminous coal that burns with a bright flame, used for making oils and gas
claes	clothing
coo	cow
creels	baskets
cures	characters
deputy	a man who deals with safety arrangements in a coal pit
ee	you
face pans	conveyors from the coal face
fireman	a man who explodes charges in a pit or mine and deals with safety: a deputy
flet	flat
forbye	besides
forrit	forward

Glossary

gaun	go, going
grieve	overseer, foreman
hutch	a small waggon for moving coal from the face
jewel	a high grade coal with a clear, shining surface
kail blades	coal and blaes laminated, a good burning coal for both domestic and industrial use
ken	know
longjohns	long underpants
miraculous	drunk
muckle	big
oncost	a time-worker
oo	we
oversman	overseer, senior to a deputy, but junior to an under-manager
pan runs	a longwall coal face using pans to remove the coal
parrot	a highly volatile bituminous coal which ignites easily and burns with a clear bright flame and a crackling sound
penny aboot	see explanation by Peter Herriot, above, p. 100
redd	waste
semmit	vest
skin the cat	swing through a complete circle
splint	a hard coarse splintering coal that burns with great heat
stent	allotted task or ground to be worked
syver	street drain
tatties	potatoes
tree	pit prop
tree-drawing	pulling out pit props
tubs	hutches or small waggons for coal
verra	very
wir	our